Focus on Grammar

WORKBOOK

An **ADVANCED** Course for Reference and Practice

Rachel Spack Koch

Longman

**Focus on Grammar: An Advanced Course
for Reference and Practice Workbook**

Editorial Director: Joanne Dresner
Development Editor: Randee Falk
Production Editor: Andrea West
Production Management: Circa 86
Text Design: Six West Design
Cover Design: A Good Thing

ISBN 201-65695-7

1 2 3 4 5 6 7 8 9 10-CRS-9998979695

Contents

About the Author

Rachel Spack Koch has taught ESL, developed ESL materials, and served as grammar coordinator at the University of Miami for more than twenty years. She has also taught ESL at Harvard University, at Bellevue Community College, and at Miami-Dade Community College. In addition to *Focus on Grammar: An Advanced Course for Reference and Practice Workbook,* she has contributed to other widely used ESL workbooks and has written structure and writing questions for the TOEFL. Currently, she serves as comonitor of the ENGL-SL student list, a global educational interchange for students and teachers on the Internet.

1. Using Verb Tenses

Complete the following article by filling in the blanks with the correct form of the verbs in parentheses.

When people think of the stereotypic American, what

_____*do*_____ they imagine? They usually _____
   1. (do / did)   2. (picture / are picturing)

a pleasant, big, blond football player, whose ancestors

_____ in the New World from northern Europe in the
   3. (arrived / have arrived)

eighteenth or early nineteenth century. While a great number of

Americans do descend from northern Europeans, the population is

actually made up of groups from all over the world. Large numbers of

southern and eastern Europeans _____ to arrive in the
                                   4. (have begun / began)

United States before the end of the nineteenth century; thus, there are

now, for example, many well-established Italian, Greek, Portuguese,

Polish, and Armenian communities. Asians _____ to
                                            5. (have begun / had begun)

immigrate even before then. In recent decades, other Asians

and people from Central and South America and the Caribbean

_____ in large numbers. Like earlier immigrants,
6. (have been arriving / had been arriving)

these new immigrants often _____ their own
                              7. (establish / used to establish)

communities.

With the waves of immigrants _____ new
                               8. (came / were coming)

languages, customs, and foods. Especially in recent years,

Italian, Mexican, Chinese, Thai, and Japanese restaurants

_____ all over the country; pizza, fajitas, and chow
9. (have sprung up / had sprung up)

mein, which _____ considered foreign dishes, are now
               10. (used to be / would be)

(continued on next page)

as American as apple pie. Many Spanish words—for example, *amigo, siesta, adiós,* and *macho*—

_____ an integral part of most Americans' vocabulary.
11. (have become / become)

It appears that the "stereotypic" American _____ in reality. The real
12. (doesn't exist / isn't existing)

American is an amalgam of many cultures. In the past, people thought that various groups

_____ into one culture, but in fact, the opposite _____:
13. (will assimilate / would assimilate)   14. (has occurred / would have occurred)

There are many and varied cultural expressions. In the future, this cultural variety

_____ even more evident. In the future, Americans _____
15. (is / will be)   16. (will have spoken / will be speaking)

with more vocabulary from more languages, and they _____ foods
17. (are cooking / will be cooking)

from all over the world. By the mid-twenty-first century, the so-called stereotype

_____ even less accurate than it is today.
18. (has become / will have become)

2. Using Verb Tenses

*Read the following essay about an immigrant family. Complete the essay by
filling in the blanks with the correct form of the verbs in parentheses.*

My parents and I came to live in the United States when I was five years old. Although my family is now very comfortable, at first we had a hard time adjusting to life here. We *had thought* that
1. (had thought / were thinking)

everybody in America _____
2. (was / has been)

very rich. Imagine our surprise when we

_____ that it was hard for
3. (learned / were learning)

many people, my father included, to make a living. My

father _____ as
4. (had been working / has been working)

a dentist in Europe before we _____
5. (have come / came)

here twenty years ago. Here he couldn't work as a dentist

right away because he _____
6. (hadn't been passing / hadn't passed)

the state examinations yet. While he _____

_____ for the dentist examinations, he
7. (had studied / was studying)

_____ in a dental laboratory in
8. (worked / has worked)

order to support his family.

Within a year, he _____
9. (was passing / had passed)

the examinations and _____
10. (has been establishing / had established)

himself in practice with a local dentist. He

_____ here for twenty years
11. (has been practicing / was practicing)

now and _____ some recognition.
12. (was gaining / has gained)

On the fifteenth of next month, his colleagues

_____ a dinner to honor him for
13. (are having / have)

his work with poor immigrants.

My mother, too, _____
14. (was / has been)

happy here. She _____ a degree in
15. (has been getting / got)

finance five years ago and now _____
16. (is owning / owns)

and _____ her own profitable copy
17. (operating / operates)

center. She _____ courses
18. (has been taking / had been taking)

for a long time before she actually _____
19. (got / had gotten)

her degree; she took only one or two courses a semester

because she was busy looking after my father, my brother,

and me. Now she is an independent woman who not only

_____ her own business but
20. (ran / runs)

is thinking about expanding it. As soon as she

_____ some suitable investors, she
21. (will find/finds)

_____ some franchises.
22. (is going to set up / sets up)

I myself _____ a
23. (have been having / had)

wonderful life. Last year I _____
24. (got / have gotten)

my law degree, and since then I _____
25. (have been working / was working)

_____in a small law firm where I am very

happy. I think that within five years, I _____
26. (will be/would be)

a partner in the firm. I know I _____
27. (work / will be working)

at least ten hours a day during that time, but it's OK

because I love my work. At the end of five years, I

_____ myself as a
28. (will have established / have established)

competent professional, and I hope to enjoy the benefits

of this success for a long time to come.

My family and I faced some difficulties when we

first _____ here because we
29. (arrived / were arriving)

_____ things to be easier than
30. (had expected / have expected)

they in fact were. But we have all succeeded beyond our

wildest dreams and are looking forward to even more

success. When I _____, I know I
31. (die / will die)

_____ a good and rewarding life.
32. (will have lived / will live)

3. Using Tenses in Sentences with Future Time Clauses

Elections were held by a high school graduating class for the following distinctions which were won by the people listed. The results appeared in the school yearbook, along with an article projecting the future for these winners. Complete the article by filling in the blanks with the correct forms of the verbs in parentheses.

Most Likely to Succeed	Al Albert
Funniest	Ed Edelman
Most Athletic	Fred Fenson
Best Dressed	Gail George
Most Popular	Harry Hernández
Cleverest	Katherine Klumper
Class Sweethearts	Rose Rincón and Bob Bradley

Here's what we can expect from some of our graduating seniors in the next decade.

There is no doubt that Al Albert will be a fine lawyer. Whenever famous criminals _____need_____ the best legal defense, Al _____ there in court. Our class comedian, Ed Edelman, will no doubt be the most popular of the stand-up comics. When the television industry _____ prizes to its best comedy stars, Ed certainly _____ one. The

1. (need)
2. (be)
3. (give)
4. (win)

Most Valuable Player of the American League? Fred Fenson _____ the award for being the best player of the year as soon as he _____ a team.

5. (receive)
6. (join)

Since she is the best-dressed person in our graduating class, it's no surprise that Gail George has accepted a job at *Gorgeous Magazine*. Once people see her work, she undoubtedly

_____ well known in
7. (be)
the fashion field. As the most

popular in our class, Harry

Hernández, whatever he

_____ and wherever
8. (do)
he _____, surely
9. (go)
_____ friends. And our
10. (have)
clever Katherine Klumper? She is

going to be a financial wizard. After

she _____ Cornell
11. (enter)
University this fall as a sophomore,

she _____ both her
12. (get)
B.A. and M.B.A. within three

years. There are two people we

feel especially fond of: Rose Rincón

and Bob Bradley, our class

sweethearts. They have been going

together for five years; we know

that they _____ a
13. (have)
lifetime of happiness after they

_____ married next
14. (get)
month.

So, what _____
15. (we / all / do)
during the next ten years? What

careers will we be participating in?

How will we fare as spouses and

parents? Stay in touch, and come

to our tenth class reunion. By that

time, we _____, studying,
16. (work)
and/or keeping house for ten years.

So when we _____
17. (get)
together for our reunion, we

certainly _____ a lot to
18. (have)
talk about!

4. Using Verb Tenses

This conversation occurred at a high school reunion that took place ten years after graduation. Circle the letter of the phrase or phrases that would complete the sentences correctly.

A: Al Albert

B: Bob Bradley

1. **A:** Hi, Bob! Great to see you!

   B: Great to see you, too, Al. What _____ for these past ten years?

   A. did you do

   B. have you done

   C. have you been doing

   D. are you doing

2. **A:** Well, I _____ my medical training. I _____ my first job as a doctor in two weeks, on July 1.

   A. will have finished/start

   B. 've just finished/'m starting

   C. just finish/'ve started

   D. had finished/start

   B: Oh. So you're a doctor. I thought you were studying law.

3. **A:** You have a good memory. I _____ law, but I decided to study medicine instead.

   A. studied

   B. have studied

   C. will have studied

   D. was going to study

4. **A:** What about you?

   B: I write television scripts. That is, I write them but I _____ them. So far, _____ only one.

        A. don't sell/I've sold

        B. didn't sell/I've been selling

        C. hadn't sold/I had sold

        D. won't sell/I sell

5. **A:** Well, I know it takes a while to catch on. You were always a really funny guy in high school. I'll

   bet you write funny scripts.

   B: As a matter of fact, I _____ comedy. I'm getting discouraged, though. I just hope that one

   day an important producer _____ just one of the forty-seven scripts I've written.

        A. have been writing/will like

        B. had been writing/would have liked

        C. will write/would like

        D. wrote/used to like

6. **A:** Don't despair! A producer _____ one of your scripts very soon. Do you remember Jenny

   Lee? Eleven publishers _____ her novel, and then just last week, Brown-Smith Publishers

   accepted it.

        A. is picking up/have rejected

        B. is going to pick up/had rejected

        C. will pick up/were rejecting

        D. picks up/rejected

7. **B:** I'm sure that she _____ delighted.

        A. would be

        B. is

        C. has been

        D. will have been

(continued on next page)

8. **A:** Of course. Now, tell me about you and Rose. Do you have any children?

   B: Oh, Rose and I _____ married only for two years. _____ married to Melissa now.

       A. are/I've been

       B. were/I'm

       C. have been/I'm

       D. had been/I was

9. **A:** You _____ divorced from Rose? I'm sorry.

   B: It's OK. We're both better off. You would like Melissa. She's studying medicine, by the way.

       A. get

       B. were getting

       C. got

       D. used to get

10. **A:** Really? Does she know what her specialty _____?

    B: Psychiatry.

        A. would be

        B. was

        C. has been

        D. is going to be

11. **A:** What a coincidence! That's my specialty, too.

    B: Great! Let's get together. _____ dinner at our house. We can talk about our professional futures.

        A. We'll all have

        B. We'd all have

        C. We'll have had

        D. We'd all be having

12. **A:** Sure. And our carefree pasts. Do you remember how our biggest worry _____ whether we

_____ a date on Saturday night?

B: Right. Those were the good old days!

    A. had been/used to have

    B. used to be/would have

    C. would be/used to have

    D. was/have had

5. Using Verb Tenses

The murder trial of Jesse Jones is being broadcast live on TV. Because of technical difficulties, some of the verbs cannot be heard. Complete the sentences with the correct form of the verbs in parentheses. More than one form may be possible.

We are here in the Washington County Courthouse at the trial of Jesse Jones, who is accused of

murdering his wife. We _____*are waiting*_____ now for today's session to begin. As you know,

1. (wait)

Jones has pleaded innocent to this horrendous charge. Today, we _____ the

                        2. (hear)

testimony of his mother, who will probably claim that Jesse always _____ a good

                        3. (be)

little boy and that he _____ her every day since the day fifteen years ago when he

            4. (telephone)

_____ home. Yesterday, you remember, Jesse Jones's fifth-grade teacher

5. (leave)

_____ quite a different story; she _____ that when Jesse was in her

6. (tell)   7. (testify)

class, he _____ the other children's pencils and money all the time.

    8. (steal)

This morning we heard the testimony of Jones's good friend, Harry Bliss, who

_____ that he and Jones _____ to play tennis together at 7:00 P.M. on

9. (say)   10. (go)

August 21, the night of the murder. They _____ for about half an hour, he said, when

                     11. (play)

they _____ in the middle of a game because Harry's bad knee _____

    12. (stop)   13. (hurt)

him again. They then drove to a nearby fast-food place for a hamburger before going to Jesse Jones's

home, where they _____ his wife dead on the floor at about 8:30 P.M.

       14. (find)

This is in direct contrast to the testimony of a neighbor of the Joneses, who said that he

_____ Jesse Jones and his wife, Madelaine, together at 8:00 P.M. At that time, from about

15. (see)

7:50 to 8:05, Jesse and Madelaine Jones _____ very loud, possibly even having an

                16. (talk)

argument, the neighbor said. Then they both _____ into the house.

                  17. (go)

(continued on next page)

Now, here comes the judge, the Honorable Sheldon O'Malley. We _____

18. (waiting)

expectantly for more than an hour for his appearance! In a few minutes, today's session of the trial will

commence. Oh, what's that? The judge _____ something now. Well, ladies and

19. (say)

gentlemen, it now _____ that today's session of this trial is going to be postponed.

20. (seem)

The defendant's lawyer _____ one extra day to call a very important witness to the

21. (request)

stand. He says this witness will prove the innocence of his client.

Stay tuned, ladies and gentlemen. We will have some astute courtroom observations for you

from our experts right after this commercial announcement. And tomorrow at this time, I know that

you _____ the mystery witness on this channel, when he or she speaks from the

22. (watch)

witness stand. By the end of the day tomorrow, I think that we already _____ where

23. (learn)

Jesse Jones *really* was on the night of August 21.

6. Editing

Read this student's letter. Find and correct the twenty errors in verb tense usage.

Dear Ricardo,

       have been

    I ~~am~~ here in the United States for three weeks now. Classes in my intensive English program

in Chicago have begun last Tuesday. Every day, the teachers had given homework. Last night, while I wrote

my composition, someone has knocked on the door. It was a mistake. It has been someone looking for a

different apartment. I was hoping it has been someone looking for me. I feel very lonely. I think that nobody

is caring about a lonely student from far away.

    Also, the food here is really terrible. I am thinking that I am going to lose a lot of weight because I

don't eat much. The weather is bad, too. It is raining every day. The people are being rude. And I often am

not understanding them. My mother has written me a nice letter last week, but she hadn't sent me any

money with the letter.

    Basically, things here are worse than I thought they will be. The stereotypic American is fun-loving

and friendly, right? It hadn't been that way at all for me. I didn't meet any friendly people yet, and I

certainly hadn't been having any fun.

    I'll be very happy to be home again next year. By this time next year, I have finished my studies

forever, and I'll work in my family's business. I can't wait to be home again!

    Please write soon.

        Your friend Marco

7. Personalization

Write a brief history of your life, using some of the phrases in the box.

When I was born, my family…

While I was in school,…

After graduating from high school,…

Since then,…

Every year,…

Right now,…

By the end of next year,…

In _____ years,…

By the time I am old,…

_____

_____

_____

_____

_____

_____

_____

_____

_____

_____

_____

_____

_____

_____

1. Using Modal Expressions of Necessity

The following is information provided by The Diet Center, a place where people go to lose weight and become fit. Complete the information by filling in the blanks with the correct form in parentheses.

The Diet Center

People who want to benefit from our program

__must not__ eat junk food. In order to benefit, they
1. (must not / don't have to)

_____ eat only the food prescribed by the Center. This
2. (should / might)

food is tasty; contrary to what many people think, food that is healthy

_____ taste terrible. Vitamins are recommended for
3. (must not / doesn't have to)

program participants, but participants _____ take
4. (needn't / shouldn't)

them.

The program has certain rules about exercise. Participants

_____ exercise at least three times a week and
5. (have to / might)

_____ exercise at least 30 minutes each time. In fact,
6. (must / could)

participants _____ exercise five times a week if
7. (should / are to)

possible, but this is not a program requirement.

Is our program right for you? You _____ try
8. (should / are to)

it out. The decision to join is yours. But once you join, you

_____ follow the rules, or you won't get your money's
9. (might / had better)

worth.

Using Modal Expressions of Certainty

John Atkins and his friend Bob have gone to the airport to meet John's wife. Complete the conversation by filling in the blanks with the correct form in parentheses.

John: Jane's flight was coming in at 6:00, and it's 6:30 now. She _____*should*_____ be here already.
1. (could / should)

Bob: She _____ be. The arrivals board shows her flight is delayed and hasn't
2. (can't / may not)

landed yet.

John: Oh, no! The plane _____ be having mechanical problems. I hope not.
3. (could / should)

Bob: You're just getting nervous. These delays are never because of serious problems. There

_____ be some less serious reason. For example, there _____
4. (must / is to)   5. (should / could)

be a delay because a lot of other flights are coming in now.

[An hour later:]

John: I think everyone's gotten off, and I don't see Jane. But she called me from the airport right

before her flight. She _____ possibly have missed the plane.
6. (must not / couldn't)

Bob: No, I'm sure she didn't. She was on the plane, so there _____ be more people
7. (must / must not)

getting off. Look—here's Jane now.

John: You're right. And look at those circles under her eyes! She's totally exhausted! She

_____ gotten a lot of sleep on the plane. That's terrible on an overnight flight.
8. (couldn't have / should not have)

3. Using Modal Expressions in Statements about the Past

Jane Payne has had a lonely evening and has written about it in her diary. Complete the diary entry by filling in the blanks with the correct form in parentheses.

I wanted to go to Martha's party for our class tonight, but I didn't want to go alone. All my classmates

had made other plans and wouldn't go with me. Charles couldn't go. He said that he wanted to go but

couldn't because he _____*had to study*_____ for a chemistry test on Monday. Cecilia actually
1. (had to study / must have studied)

did go to the party, but she went with her boyfriend. I guess that they didn't want me to be a fifth

wheel. She really _____ home to study for the test, though, because she
2. (must have stayed / should have stayed)

doesn't get good grades in chemistry and she needs to. I _____ to
3. (might have gone / must have gone)

the party with Bill, but yesterday afternoon he ended up in the hospital with an appendicitis

(continued on next page)

attack, so of course he couldn't go. Irving _____ go to Cleveland
4. (must have had to / might have had to)

for the weekend, because his sister was getting married there, so he wasn't available.

Rudolph _____ me to take me to the party, but he never did.
5. (was supposed to call / must have called)

Jackie, my so-called best friend in class, _____ to make
6. (was to telephone / had better have telephoned)

arrangements to go together to the party, too, but she never called, either. And Mary

_____ about the party, as she is sometimes very forgetful. It
7. (may have forgotten / should have forgotten)

_____ that everybody was avoiding me; everybody really
8. (couldn't have been / wasn't supposed to be)

_____ busy.
9. (must have been / should have been)

4. Using Modal Expressions

This conversation occurred at a ten-year high school reunion. Circle the letter of the phrase or phrases that would complete the sentences correctly.

A: Amanda Albright

B: Barbara Balms

1. **A:** Barbara! Guess who I just ran into! Al Albert!

   B: No! Where is he? Gee, I remember how you used to talk about him all the time. You really _____

   in love with him during our senior year.

   A. must have been

   B. should have been

   C. have been

   D. have to be

2. **A:** I certainly was. I think that I _____ him.

   B: Really?

   A. used to marry

   B. may have married

   C. could have married

   D. must have married

3. **A:** Yes, I was that serious about him. But then he took Deirdre out, and I got angry and broke off with him. Now, after all these years, I still regret it.

   B: Do you think that you _____ start something up again?

      A. are to

      B. had better

      C. must be able to

      D. might be able to

4. **A:** I don't know. Well, I'm going to invite him to dinner. I think that by now his manners _____.

      A. must improve

      B. must have improved

      C. have got to improve

      D. can't have improved

5. **B:** Amanda! He _____ married! You don't even know whether or not he's available.

      A. should be

      B. has got to be

      C. had better be

      D. might be

6. **A:** I can find that out easily enough. And who knows? By this time next year, Al and I _____ the knot, after all these years. I've always known he's the only man for me.

      A. have to tie

      B. must have tied

      C. should have tied

      D. may have tied

7. **B:** Amanda, you surely _____ that for ten years you've thought only of Al!

      A. may not mean

      B. might not mean

      C. can't mean

      D. shouldn't mean

(continued on next page)

8. **A:** Well, not exactly. But now that I see him, I know I have to get together with him again. I _____

this long ago.

       A. must have done

       B. should have done

       C. had to do

       D. may have done

9. **B:** But what if he's forgotten about you? What if he no longer cares for you?

  A: Oh, he _____ about me, and I think he still cares for me.

       A. may not be forgotting

       B. could not have forgotten

       C. should not have forgotten

       D. might not be forgetting

10. **B:** Well, good luck, Amanda. You are so successful in everything you do that you _____ his

heart without any trouble at all.

       A. must capture

       B. are to capture

       C. should capture

       D. have got to

5. Using Modal Expressions in Statements about the Present and Future

The Messer family is not in good financial shape. To understand their situation, look at their balance sheet for this past year. Then read the plan of advice for the Messers that follows on the next page, and complete the sentences by filling in the blanks with a form that expresses the idea indicated in parentheses. In most cases more than one answer is possible. There are two degrees of certainty: quite certain and possible. There are four degrees of necessity: absolutely necessary, strongly advised, advised, and suggested.

INCOME		
John's salary as architect	$ 60,300	
Withdrawal from savings	32,800	
Loans	6,500	
Helen's salary as part-time secretary	10,100	
	109,700	
OUTGO		
Food		20,000
Taxes		19,700
Loan payments		12,200
Mortgage payments		9,700
Home repairs		6,000
Insurance		8,500
Auto upkeep, two cars		5,800
Utilities, telephone		5,200
Clothing		9,600
Travel and entertainment		7,400
Miscellaneous		5,000
		109,100
ASSETS		
House	129,000	
Checking, savings	3,000	
Retirement account	11,000	
	143,000	
LIABILITIES		
Mortgage		86,000
Credit-card debt		10,800
Personal loans		8,000
		104,800

(continued on next page)

The Messers _____*had better take*_____ some action right away; if they don't, they will soon
1. (*strongly advised* — take)

be totally bankrupt. This year the Messers had enough money to meet their expenses, but only

because they used almost all their savings and borrowed from friends. In order to keep from total

financial devastation, they are going to need to take strong steps. They _____ a
2. (*absolutely necessary* — make)

plan to spend less money than they make. This is obligatory.

They can accomplish this in a number of ways. To begin with, they _____
3. (*suggested* — cut)

their food bills by more than 50 percent by eating at home all of the time instead of eating in

restaurants so often. Another item which they _____ back on is clothing; their
4. (*suggested* — cut)

clothing bill can probably be halved, too. Then, $7,400 is too much money for a couple in debt to

spend on travel and entertainment; the Messers _____ vacations for two years.
5. (*advised* — eliminate)

They also don't _____ have two cars; they can cut their car expenses in half
6. (*absolutely necessary* — have)

if one of them uses public transportation regularly. The biggest part of their income goes toward

paying off loans. One thing they _____ is to refinance the loans.
7. (*suggested* — do)

At the same time that they are going to spend less, they _____ the
8. (*absolutely necessary* — make)

money that they have earns more interest. With the aid of a competent advisor, they

_____ the little money that they do have in places where they will get more
9. (*advised* — invest)

interest safely. Mr. Messer _____ an effort to earn more money, either by
10. (*absolutely necessary* — make)

bringing in more clients to his architectural firm or by getting a promotion. Mrs. Messer,

too, _____ more than she is earning now, but to do this, first she
11. (*absolutely necessary* — earn)

_____ a better education. It will be difficult for her to advance in the firm
12. (*absolutely necessary* — get)

where she is presently working; she _____ to work in another firm and go to
13. (*possible* — need)

school at night.

The Messers _____ it difficult to spend less. But by exerting all their
14. (*possible* — find)

self-discipline and keeping their goal in mind, they _____ solvent again within
15. (*quite certain* — become)

two years.

6. Editing

Read the following letter from Alice to Bruce. Find and correct the eighteen errors in the forms of the modals and modal-like expressions.

My dearest Bruce,

I have been thinking long and hard about our problems. You must ~~to~~ be very upset, and I am, too. I really want to work out our problems.

First, I have apologize about the dog. I really shouldn't had had your dog put to sleep, in spite of the fact that you were suppose to do that. Then, seeing the new puppy must have upsetting you a lot. I was so angry about our situation that I couldn't had been thinking clearly.

Then, I think I've got find a job, not because you aren't a good provider, but because my having some money of my own should takes some pressure off you. I should to find something part-time, something that I could to do at home, like telephone sales.

About the housekeeping, I will make amends, but here is where you can help. You could have pick up your things, including towels, and help clean up the dinner dishes. You might have offer to help out with folding the laundry—we could to do it together. Actually, it might been fun!

On your part, I ask only that you center your life around home. That's all. You've to be home for dinner and has to stay home most evenings.

I will do everything possible to make life pleasant for you around here. We must to take control of our situation and make our marriage wonderful again, like it used to being. I really think it is worth everything.

Your loving wife,

Alice

7. Personalization

*Most people readily see one or two big mistakes they have made in their lives.
What do you think is the most serious mistake that you have made in your
life? What would the right action have been? Write a short essay. Begin the
essay with this sentence:* **The most serious mistake of my life was...**
Include some of the phrases in the box.

> I shouldn't have...
>
> Instead, I should have...
>
> I could have...
>
> Because of that mistake, I had to...
>
> In the future, I have to...
>
> In the future, I should...

_____

_____

_____

_____

_____

_____

_____

_____

_____

_____

_____

_____

_____

_____

_____

1. Using Auxiliary Verb *Do* for Emphasis

Read Bruce's response to Alice's letter. Fill in the blanks with the appropriate emphatic forms for the verbs, keeping the same tense.

My dearest Alice,

    I received your letter, and I must say it

____*did touch*____ me deeply. I want you to
1. (touched)

know that I really love you very much and

_____ to work out our problems.
2. (want)

    While it is true that I _____
3. (became)

angry about the dog, I am sorry about it. We

could have discussed that problem reasonably,

as I hope we can discuss anything else. The

house has been quite messy for a long time, but

I noticed that you _____ very
4. (cleaned up)

thoroughly last week; I want you to know

that I _____ to be more helpful with
5. (intend)

chores around the house in the future. I am

also planning to be here every night.

    It may be difficult at first, but we

_____ start communicating again,
6. (have to)

just as you have said. If we _____,
7. (communicate)

I believe we will be happy together again,

just as we used to be.

    Your loving husband,

    Bruce

2. Using Auxiliary Verb *Do* for Emphasis Where Possible

*Read the following notes taken by a marriage counselor. Fill in the blanks with
appropriate emphatic forms with **do** or **did** where possible or with other
appropriate forms where emphatic forms are not possible.*

CLIENT: _____

DATE: _____

NOTES:

Today, after one month, I saw Bruce and Alice again. The situation is

very much improved. Last week, Alice actually _____*did apologize*_____
                                                      1. (apologize)

for the dog incidents, and Bruce accepted that apology graciously.

Alice actually _____ to clean up the house daily and
                  2. (begin)

reports that now Bruce _____ his appreciation quite
                           3. (express)

regularly. The most important fact: two weeks ago, Bruce

_____ to stay home for dinner and evenings, and
     4. (agree)

now he _____ with the household chores every day.
          5. (help)

We _____ of Alice's mother, briefly, at the beginning
      6. (speak)

of our session, but very little progress has been made. This

_____ indeed a sensitive subject with her. However,
     7. (be)

Bruce _____ more aware of this now, and I think that
          8. (be)

in the future, he _____ Alice some encouragement to
                     9. (be going to give)

loosen the ties to her mother, which would be appropriate.

I _____ encouraged by the progress Bruce and Alice
     10. (feel)

have made. We shall meet again in one month, when, hopefully, they

will have successfully developed a new routine based on their good

intentions. This couple _____ a good chance for a
                            11. (have)

bright future, and with effort on both their parts, I think that it

_____ .
  12. (be going to happen)

3. Using *Be* and *Do* for Contrast Where Possible

Complete the following statements of general knowledge by filling in the blanks with the appropriate verb forms, using contrastive forms where possible.

1. Christopher Columbus didn't land in Florida, but he _____*did land*_____ in Santo Domingo not too far away.

2. Even though many of the early settlers didn't survive the first year in Massachusetts, about half of them _____ and celebrated the first Thanksgiving with the local Indians.

3. Alaska is not the most populous state, but it _____ the largest in area.

4. People don't eat as much meat as they used to, but they _____ more fish.

5. Not all Americans vote in elections, but many _____.

6. Many adults don't know how to use computers or VCRs, but most children _____ to use these things.

7. Benjamin Franklin was never a president of the United States, but he _____ a very important statesman.

8. Even though dogs and cats don't understand the words people speak to them, they _____ when people are angry at them.

9. Green Bay, Wisconsin, doesn't have a baseball team, but it _____ a famous football team.

4. Editing

Read the following article. Find and correct the seven errors in the forms of the verbs used for emphasis or contrast. In making your corrections, use emphatic/contrastive forms.

World of Witchcraft

ll over the world people believe in superstitions without knowing why they ~~are believe~~ *do believe* in them or what exactly the superstitions are about. For example, the good luck associated with a rabbit's foot has nothing to do with the

(continued on next page)

rabbit or the foot itself; the good luck actually does relates to the quality of fecundity, or having many offspring, which people considered to be a sign of good fortune.

In many cultures, people say "God bless you" or similar words when someone sneezes; in past centuries, they actually did believed that sneezing meant death was coming, so God's blessing for the sneezer was, in fact, a prayer for continued life.

The number thirteen is considered unlucky in many places. The history of this superstition goes back to Norse mythology, when a thirteenth guest, uninvited, crashed a dinner party of twelve gods, causing the death of the most beloved god, Balder. It is perhaps strange that the number thirteen is considered unlucky in the United States. In American history thirteen doesn't represent anything bad, but it is represent something good: the original thirteen colonies.

Also widely regarded as a symbol of bad luck is the black cat. Originally a sign of good luck during the Middle Ages, cats became identified with lonely old women who fed them, and then with witches. Cats, while not dangerous, did became greatly feared in those days.

What about the superstitions regarding spilled salt? Throughout history, salt has been highly valued as a seasoning, preservative, and medicine, so much so, in fact, that it was used as payment for soldiers in ancient Rome. Salt was too valuable to spill, and when by accident a diner did spilled it, the custom of throwing a tiny bit over one's left shoulder was supposed to nullify the bad luck that could come with such wastefulness.

Leonardo da Vinci's famous painting, *The Last Supper,* depicted two bad omens: the spilling of salt and thirteen guests at a table. It is no wonder that these two superstitions still does remain among the most observed in the world.

5. Personalization

Write about your study of English. Include some of the phrases in the box.

> When I came to this country, I didn't speak much English, but now I . . .
>
> Although my English was limited, I . . .
>
> I *did* . . .
>
> I *was* . . .
>
> While I don't understand 100 percent of what I hear, I . . .
>
> I haven't finished my studies yet, but I . . .
>
> I *do* . . .
>
> I *am* . . .
>
> My English isn't perfect yet, but it . . .

_____

_____

_____

_____

_____

_____

_____

_____

_____

_____

_____

_____

_____

_____

_____

_____

4

Non-Count Nouns: Count and Non-Count Use

▼

PART II: THE NOUN PHRASE: SELECTED TOPICS

1. Identifying Count and Non-Count Nouns

In the following passage, write **NC** *or* **C** *to indicate whether the nouns in italics are used as count or non-count in their contexts.*

                           NC

    Why does *language* provide such a fascinating object of *study*? Perhaps because of its unique role in capturing the *breadth* of human *thought* and *endeavor.* We look around us and are awed by the variety of several thousand *languages* and *dialects,* expressing a multiplicity of worldviews, *literatures,* and ways of life. We look back at the *thoughts* of our predecessors, and find we can see only as far as *language* lets us see.

    We look forward in *time,* and find we can plan only through *language.* We look outward in *space,* and send symbols of *communication* along with our spacecraft, to explain who we are, in case there is anyone out there who wants to know.*

> *The passage is taken from David Crystal, *The Cambridge Encyclopedia of Language* (Cambridge: Cambridge University Press, 1987).

2. Identifying Non-Count Nouns

Read the following article, which discusses the livability of various places in the United States. Underline the twenty-three non-count nouns in the article.

    For all-around pleasant living conditions, people currently consider Raleigh/Durham, North Carolina, the best area in the United States. Other places also received high ratings in various categories. For example, Rochester, Minnesota, is desirable because of its excellent facilities for <u>health</u>, transportation, and education and its low level of crime and violence. San Jose, California, has the best weather, and Albuquerque, New Mexico, the best opportunities for pleasant housing. The economic situation, surprisingly, is the best in Sioux Falls, North Dakota, though Sioux Falls does not rate high in accessibility to plays, concerts, and other cultural events. Not surprisingly,

Stamford, Connecticut, an area near New York City, rates very high in this last category. For outdoor activities, Seattle is a clear winner; its location near the ocean and mountains offers many opportunities for hiking, skiing, sailing and other water sports, and overall enjoyment of nature.

The cities were rated on 23 factors. People's concerns about safety make a lack of crime and violence a top priority. Other strong considerations include the availability of clean water, clean air, low taxes, good schools, opportunities for employment and job growth, inexpensive living, and proximity to a big city as well as to wilderness areas.*

* Information is taken from *Money,* September 1994.

3. Using Noun Plus *of* before Normally Non-Countable Nouns

Complete the letter by choosing a phrase from the box. Some phrases will be used more than once, and in some places more than one phrase is appropriate.

a serving of	a piece of	a slice of
a game of	a glass of	a flash of
a clap of	a period of	a branch of

Dear Mary,

You know how much I dislike picnics. Ted insisted that we go on one before the summer ended, and although I resisted, I am so glad that we finally did that. First, he did all the work. He wouldn't let me do ____*a piece of*____ work. Of
1.
course, he wouldn't even accept _____ advice from me, either.
2.

We drove off on Saturday morning to Grover's Cove, which is a pleasant, secluded area where we met three other couples. At first the weather was fine. We decided to have _____ volleyball before lunch. But our friends had
3.
forgotten the net, so we forgot about the volleyball game and sat down to play

_____ cards and drink _____ lemonade.
4.   5.

(continued on next page)

At lunch, as usual, I ate too much. I had _____ Sheila's special
6.
seven-grain bread, _____ Ted's delicious curried chicken salad,
7.
_____ Saga bleu cheese, _____ Sheila's famous apple pie,
8.   9.
and _____ cranberry juice. We settled in to listen to _____
10.   11.
music by Mozart, the Violin Concerto #3, on the portable CD player that Robert had

brought. Robert's son, by the way, has just gotten his degree in micropaleontology,

which is _____ geology. Just as we were dozing off comfortably on our
12.
blankets, we heard _____ thunder, which really startled us. Then we
13.
saw _____ lightning nearby, so we packed up hurriedly and got into
14.
our cars fast. When we turned on the car radio, we heard _____ news:
15.
tornadoes were in the area, and it was going to be dangerous to be outside for

_____ time.
16.

We were quite anxious, but we made it home safely and stayed together

singing old songs for the rest of the afternoon. We really had a wonderful day. I'm

sorry you weren't with us.

Love,

Shelley

4. **Using Count and Non-Count Nouns**

Read the following article reporting the results of a survey that asked people what they valued most in life. Fill in the blanks in the article, choosing between the forms given.

Survey Results

As expected, ___*good health*___ was cited as the number one factor
1. (good health / a good health)

necessary to have a happy life. Having

_____ to share the ups
2. (partner / a partner)

and downs of life was the next most

important factor. In describing what

they valued or would value in the

partner, people said they wanted to

spend their lives with someone who

had _____, who wasn't
3. (integrity / an integrity)

afraid of _____ but at the
4. (work / a work)

same time was capable of having

_____, and who would
5. (great fun / a great fun)

give _____ generously.
6. (love / a love)

Interestingly, more men than women

mentioned that they wanted their

partners to be intelligent. Women tended

to mention _____ as a
7. (practicality / a practicality)

feature they desired in a relationship.

The third factor mentioned, closely

following _____
8. (a compatible companion / compatible companion)

in importance, was a strong family,

cited equally by both sexes. Evidently,

people yearn for connections and

_____.
9. (warmth / a warmth)

Also high on the list was having

_____ that is fulfilling,
10. (career / a career)

_____ that provides
11. (job / a job)

satisfaction. _____ was
12. (Good salary / A good salary)

not the only consideration; most people

said that they also wanted to receive

_____ for their work.
13. (respect / a respect)

5. Using Count and Non-Count Nouns

The Ice Cream Association recently had this article in its newsletter. Complete the article by filling in the blanks with the correct form in parentheses.

Ice Cream Association Newsletter

_____Ice cream_____ is rated as
1. (An ice cream / Ice cream)
Americans' favorite dessert, and it is heavily

consumed. _____ is
2. (A production / Production)
estimated to be fifteen quarts per year for

each person in the United States, and if

sherbets and other fruit concoctions are

added, the figure jumps to twenty-three

quarts per person.

A kind of ice cream was created in

China four thousand years ago. At that point

in _____, people had just
3. (ancient history / ancient histories)
begun to get _____ from
4. (milk / milks)
farm animals, and the white liquid was a

prized commodity. _____
5. (A favorite dish / Favorite dish)
of the nobility consisted of a soft paste made

from _____, spices,
6. (overcooked rice / overcooked rices)
and milk, and the mixture was packed in

_____ to solidify. This milk
7. (snows / snow)
ice was considered to be _____
8. (a symbol / symbol)

of _____ at that time. The
9. (wealth / a wealth)
Chinese also developed various types of

desserts made from _____
10. (ices / ice)
combined with different fruits, and by the

thirteenth century many flavors of these

iced desserts were being sold on the streets

of Peking.

From China, Marco Polo brought

recipes for these wonderful desserts back to

fourteenth-century Italy. Before long, frozen

desserts traveled from Italy to France. And

when Catherine de' Medici married King

Henry II of France, she introduced into that

country a semifrozen dessert made from

_____.
11. (cream / creams).
Soon _____ to
12. (a way / way)
quickly freeze the iced cream and iced fruits

developed; by the 1560s these iced products

were very popular and sold by street

vendors in France and Italy. It is believed that these sweets were introduced to North America by the early English colonists, who made the mixture at home by placing bowls on ice mixed with _____ to

13. (salt / a salt)

create a lower freezing temperature. At the end of the nineteenth century, Italian immigrants added to the popularity of _____ made from fruits;

14. (the ices / the ice)

Italian street vendors, often accompanied by _____, quickly became a

15. (a music / music)

popular sight in cities across North America. Then, in the 1920s, an Ohio man introduced the first chocolate-covered vanilla ice cream bar on _____, calling it a

16. (stick / a stick)

"Good Humor Sucker." From this concept of good humor evolved the well-known Good Humor man, who to this day continues to drive his small musical truck up and down the streets of American towns, bringing _____ to children

17. (happiness / a happiness)

everywhere.*

* Based on Charles Panati, *Extraordinary Origins of Everyday Things* (Perennial Library, Harper & Row, 1987, revised 1989).

6. Editing

Read the following article. Find and correct the fourteen errors in the use of count and non-count nouns.

Spoken language is ^a^ wonderful thing, enabling us to communicate feelings and thoughts, to tell stories and even lies. Early in history of mankind, use of symbols to communicate ideas went one step further. It was not necessary to be in actual proximity to another human being when one could send signals by smokes or drums. But, how could this communications be kept in any permanent form?

People began to record markings on hard surfaces like a clay, using symbols to represent peoples, animals, or, later, various abstraction. Over many thousands of years, the pictures developed into different alphabet.

(continued on next page)

What would the world be like without writing and reading? How would knowledges pass from one generation to another? Yet writing and reading were not always skill to be taken for granted. In fact, until recent generations, a literacy has not been as common as it is now.

What about the future? Technology is advancing the ways we have of disseminating informations. One hundred years from now, computer literacies will be as commonplace and necessary as are simple literacy is now.

7. Personalization

People differ greatly in their likes and dislikes. How would you describe your likes and dislikes? Write about yourself. Include some of the phrases in the box.

> My favorite foods are . . .   My least favorite foods are . . .
>
> My favorite drinks are . . .   My least favorite drinks are . . .
>
> Some of my favorite activities are . . .
>
> Some of my least favorite activities are . . .
>
> Two subjects that interest me a lot are . . .
>
> Two subjects that don't interest me at all are . . .
>
> Two sports that I like are . . .
>
> Two occupations that interest me are . . .
>
> For me, the most important things in life are . . .

_____

_____

_____

_____

_____

_____

_____

1. Using Articles

In the following letter, fill in the blanks with the correct form in parentheses (0 if no article is needed.)

Dear Ricardo,

      Things have gotten better since I last wrote to you. First, I received

___*a*___ letter from my family with _____ very nice surprise in it: _____
1. (a / 0)   2. (the / a)   3. (the / a)

check for $200. _____ letter made me feel good because I thought my
                4. (A / The)

family had forgotten me, and _____ check made me feel even better. With
                               5. (the / 0)

_____ money, I went to _____ expensive restaurant downtown with
6. (the / a)   7. (an / 0)

_____ new friend. Yes, _____ new friend is _____ beautiful young
8. (the / a)   9. (the / a)   10. (the / a)

woman. If our relationship develops, I'll tell you her name in _____ next
                                   11. (the / 0)

letter I write to you. What I will tell you now is that she is _____ only
                                   12. (the / an)

daughter of _____ president of my university.
          13. (the / 0)

      _____ weather has improved, too. We haven't had _____ rain for
      14. (The / A)   15. (the / 0)

three weeks, now; I've seen _____ sun every day, and last weekend I went
                       16. (the / a)

to _____ beach and got _____ suntan.
   17. (a / 0)   18. (the / a)

      Do you know anything about _____ American football? It's
                             19. (the / 0)

_____ really rough game played by two teams with eleven people on each
20. (a / the)

team. _____ team that has _____ ball is supposed to take it into the
       21. (The / A)   22. (the / 0)

opposing team's territory and score _____ touchdown—that means they get
                            23. (the / a)

six points. At first, I didn't understand it, but I've gone to a few games and

I see that it's exciting but more dangerous than _____ game we play
                                   24. (a / the)

at home that we call football. Here they call our game _____ soccer.
                             25. (the / 0)

      My classes are going better, too. I like _____ organic chemistry
                            26. (the / 0)

and _____ computer science. I even like _____ history now; this course focuses on _____ most
   27. (the / 0)   28. (the / 0)   29. (the / 0)

important events of the twentieth century. I still don't like _____ English, though. I am just not
                                             30. (the / 0)

very good in _____ languages.
        31. (the / 0)

       Well, Ricardo, I gotta go! That's _____ American English way of saying "I have got
                                   32. (0 / the)

to go." Write me soon, OK?

            Marco

2.   Using Articles

*Read the following passage on the development of language and choose the correct
article to fill the blanks (0 if no article is needed).*

     Scholars do not agree on ___*the*___ degree of sophistication of language of the early human
                    1. (the / a)

beings; however, we can imagine how language might have developed among them. One theory of

_____ beginnings of language is described here briefly.
2. (the / 0)

    As _____ animals have the ability and need to communicate, so do _____ human beings.
        3. (the / 0)   4. (the / 0)

Primitive people, like people today, could make contact with _____ outside world by means of their
                                    5. (the / an)

five senses. They could see _____ other human beings, animals, and inanimate objects; they could
                6. (an / 0)

hear their sounds and the sounds of _____ environment. Also like animals, these early people did
                          7. (the / 0)

not live alone. They lived in _____ groups. By doing so, they avoided _____ loneliness, helped
                8. (the / 0)   9. (the / 0)

each other in the hunting and gathering of _____ food, and protected themselves from _____
                              10. (the / 0)   11. (a / 0)

danger. Group life made communication all the more important.

    Various ways to communicate developed. Primitive people used _____ sound, gestures, and
                                      12. (a / 0)

touch. _____ grunting sound might have indicated that _____ rock was too heavy to lift alone,
     13. (A / 0)   14. (the / a)

or _____ gesture might have meant "Come here" or "I'm hungry." _____ touch could have
  15. (a / 0)   16. (A / 0)

expressed _____ tenderness or love. Over time, _____ words evolved from sounds that represented
        17. (the / 0)   18. (the / 0)

objects and actions important to their lives.*

    * The passage is based on "Communication Mediums: Primitive Means" from *Compton's Encyclopedia, Online Edition,*
    downloaded from *America Online,* November 18, 1994.

3. Using the Definite Article or 0 Article with Names

*A travel agent has sent this letter to her client, along with plane and hotel tickets. Complete the letter by filling in the blanks with **the** where the definite article is needed and with **0** where the definite article is not needed.*

GLOBE TRAVEL

Dear Dorothea:

You will leave ___0___ Los Angeles at 11 P.M. You'll be flying at night, so you
1.

won't see _____ Rocky Mountains or _____ Mississippi River, which is really
2.   3.

a pity.

After you leave _____ United States, you'll be flying off the coast of _____
4.   5.

Canada, then over _____ Atlantic to _____ United Kingdom. As you fly over
6.   7.

_____ Europe, you will be able to see _____ France as you cross _____ Alps into
8.   9.   10.

_____ Switzerland. You'll land in _____ Geneva.
11.   12.

You have reservations at _____ Sheraton Hotel where the conference is. I've
13.

reserved a place for you on the post-conference tour to _____ Hungary and _____
14.   15.

Czech Republic, so you'll be able to see a little of eastern Europe. You'll be

coming home on a different route, as you requested, so that you can stop in _____
16.

Florida to see your grandmother. It's too bad you won't be able to visit _____
17.

Bahamas or _____ Dominican Republic while you're in the area, as _____
18.   19.

Caribbean is a great place to relax after the hard work you will have been doing at

the conference.

Your return flight is at 8 A.M. on Monday, the fifteenth, and you arrive home

at 10:20 A.M.

Have a great trip!

4. Using Articles

Complete the archaeologist's report about planet Green by supplying the articles
a, **an**, *and* **the** *where appropriate. Use* **0** *to indicate no article.*

SITE: _____

DATE: _____

NOTES:

Remains were found of what appears to be ___a___ large city on
1.

_____ island in _____ Northern Hemisphere. It seems that _____
2.   3.   4.

city was part of _____ advanced civilization.
5.

What we had thought was _____ sophisticated canal system has
6.

turned out to be something else entirely. _____ canals that we thought
7.

we saw contained no water but were covered with _____ hard surface.
8.

We think these were actually _____ roadways that _____ vehicles
9.   10.

traveled on. _____ vehicles had four wheels, and _____ pieces from
11.   12.

_____ thousands of them were seen. _____ shadows that we had
13.   14.

seen by telescope were actually _____ buildings, very tall buildings, that
15.

_____ population probably lived in. We found no agricultural areas,
16.

although we did find _____ large grassy space in _____ middle of
17.   18.

_____ island. We are not sure how the inhabitants obtained their food;
19.

probably they brought it by boat from _____ mainland, or over _____
20.   21.

bridge. We also found _____ parallel rows of _____ iron, perhaps
22.   23.

used for some form of _____ transportation. We suspect that the
24.

inhabitants traveled by air, too, but we didn't find _____ evidence of any
25.

type of airport or air transportation vehicles. We are not sure why

_____ area was abandoned, but maybe it was because _____ entire
26.   27.

planet was suffering from _____ severe pollution.
28.

5. Using Articles

Read Radio Station KESL's interview with popular disc jockey Nancy Stone.
Complete the interview by filling in the blanks with the correct article
(**0** = *no article*).

KESL: So, Nancy, why do you think ___*0*___ rock music is still so popular?
<u>1. (a / 0)</u>

Stone: Well, _____ rock music that I play on this station is classic and speaks to _____ people
<u>2. (the / 0)</u>   <u>3. (a / 0)</u>

everywhere. There are many variations of _____ rock, and I choose music I know
<u>4. (the / 0)</u>

people will respond to: I choose _____ best songs, those that speak to _____ heart.
<u>5. (the / 0)</u>   <u>6. (the / 0)</u>

KESL: Do you mean songs about _____ love?
<u>7. (the / 0)</u>

Stone: Yes, of course, but also songs about _____ pain and _____ friendship.
<u>8. (a / 0)</u>   <u>9. (a / 0)</u>

KESL: Who are _____ most popular artists?
<u>10. (the / 0)</u>

Stone: My show plays mostly _____ classic rock, you know, so we play a lot of the golden oldies,
<u>11. (the / 0)</u>

like the Beatles, the Rolling Stones, even Elvis.

KESL: What about _____ country music?
<u>12. (a / 0)</u>

Stone: I, personally, like _____ country music that I hear these days. _____ line between country
<u>13. (a / the)</u>   <u>14. (The / A)</u>

and rock is not as clear as it used to be. Until recently, _____ themes of country music—
<u>15. (the / 0)</u>

_____ abandonment, _____ prison, _____ driving in trucks—were not what our
<u>16. (the / 0)</u>   <u>17. (the / 0)</u>   <u>18. (a / 0)</u>

listeners liked to hear. Now, though, singers like Billy Ray Cyrus and Garth Brooks are very

popular, and _____ songs they sing are similar to rock songs.
<u>19. (the / 0)</u>

KESL: Any international songs?

Stone: Yes. We play some songs of Julio Iglesias and Milton Nascimento. They're popular singers, and

it's not necessary to speak _____ language they sing in order to appreciate them.
<u>20. (the / a)</u>

KESL: So _____ same music is appreciated all over _____ world?
<u>21. (the / a)</u>   <u>22. (the / 0)</u>

Stone: It seems so. I've heard "Love Me Tender" in elevators from _____ United States to _____
<u>23. (the / 0)</u>   <u>24. (the / 0)</u>

Europe to _____ Far East; I've heard "Hands Across the Water" on the stereo while flying over
<u>25. (the / 0)</u>

_____ Andes Mountains and over _____ Atlantic on _____ Concorde and even while
<u>26. (the / 0)</u>   <u>27. (the / 0)</u>   <u>28. (the / a)</u>

flying over _____ North Pole. Whether I stay in _____ Hilton Hotel in Chicago or _____
<u>29. (the / 0)</u>   <u>30. (the / 0)</u>   <u>31. (the / 0)</u>

Hilton Hotel in Cairo, _____ music that is played is _____ same. Culturally, you know,
  <u>32. (the / 0)</u>   <u>33. (the / 0)</u>

_____ planet is getting smaller and smaller.
<u>34. (the / a)</u>

KESL: What about Peter, Paul, and Mary or folk singers like Joan Baez?

Stone: Never. Well, almost never. _____ only time I play Peter, Paul, and Mary is at Christmas. They
  <u>35. (The / 0)</u>

recorded _____ Christmas concert at _____ end of _____ eighties that people like to
  <u>36. (a / 0)</u>   <u>37. (the / an)</u>   <u>38. (the / 0)</u>

hear during the holiday season. Joan Baez hasn't been played much since _____ period
  <u>39. (the / 0)</u>

when people were angry about _____ war in Vietnam.
  <u>40. (the / a)</u>

KESL: What about songs about _____ environment?
  <u>41. (the / 0)</u>

Stone: Not today so much as previously. There's not much you can sing about regarding _____
  <u>42. (the / an)</u>

ozone layer or _____ carbon dioxide in _____ atmosphere.
  <u>43. (the / a)</u>   <u>44. (an / the)</u>

KESL: By the way, I've heard that _____ president is _____ fan of _____ rock.
  <u>45. (the / 0)</u>   <u>46. (a / the)</u>   <u>47. (a / 0)</u>

Stone: I've heard that, too. I remember that _____ President Bush liked _____ country music,
  <u>48. (the / 0)</u>   <u>49. (the / 0)</u>

and _____ President Clinton used to like _____ song called "Chelsea Morning"; in fact, he
  <u>50. (the / 0)</u>   <u>51. (a / 0)</u>

named his daughter Chelsea because he liked _____ song so much.
  <u>52. (the / a)</u>

KESL: What's your all-time favorite, Nancy?

Stone: Oh, I don't know. Actually, I'll tell you _____ secret: I really like _____ classical music
  <u>53. (a / 0)</u>   <u>54. (the / 0)</u>

most of all.

6.   Editing

Read the following bulletin. Find and correct the twenty-one errors in the use of articles, either by supplying the correct article or by omitting the article.

METROPOLITAN ZOO

                                                              an
Your Metropolitan Zoo needs you! Can you adopt ∧ animal? You can "adopt" an animal by

contributing money for its care. By adopting an animal, you will help us keep zoo in good con-

dition with the healthy animals, and you will have a satisfaction of knowing that your love and

your efforts are keeping "your" animal alive and well. Which animal would you like to adopt?

(continued on next page)

Needing adoption right now are: two tigers, one lion, two camels, a family of three chimpanzees, and one gorilla.

Here is some information about the animals needing adoption. Both our tigers are female; we are hoping to obtain male from Pakistan next year. A lion, recently named Mufasa by a group of the schoolchildren, is three years old. Both camels are Arabian kind, with one hump, not Bactrian kind, with two humps. Chimpanzees in our zoo act just like human family. They take care of each other, laugh, and sometimes even have the arguments. We have only one gorilla now; he is most popular animal at zoo, and also most expensive to maintain. He needs several sponsors. He puts on the show every afternoon by interacting with a visitors. He loves an applause that he gets.

After you adopt, you will regularly be advised of a life situation of your animal. You will be honored at our annual spring banquet, and you will receive free admission to a zoo.

Please find it in your heart to contribute to well-being of our animals.

7. Personalization

Write a letter describing your hometown to someone who is about to visit there for the first time. Describe the character of your hometown and the most important places to see. Include some of the phrases in the boxes.

When you come to my hometown, you will first notice the atmosphere of . . .

The most prominent physical feature of my hometown is . . .

The most prominent building in my hometown is . . .

Some interesting things to see in my hometown include . . .

Be sure to visit . . .

In the evening, you can go to . . .

The people are friendly and show a lot of . . .

Near the center of town, you will find . . .

My hometown is noted for . . .

Although my hometown is new and modern, it doesn't have . . .

Fortunately/unfortunately, my hometown has/doesn't have . . .

I'm sure you will like . . .

What I miss about my hometown is . . .

UNIT

6

Modification
of Nouns

▼

1. Putting Modifiers in Appropriate Order

Complete the following review of a fashion show by filling in the blanks with the modifiers placed in their correct order. Place commas where necessary.

$\mathcal{L}$ast week at __the annual fashion__ show in Paris,
1. (fashion / the / annual)

_____ designers displayed their latest creations.
2. (young / some / bright)

Everybody had expected _____ fashions to
3. (these / spring / new)

be similar to last year's rather ordinary and boring clothes; instead,

the designers delighted the audience with a brilliant presentation.

Drawing on _____ inspirations, they showed
4. (different / many / international)

_____ collection in a decade.
5. (first / exciting / the / new)

    Maurice Isak's inspiration came from the Orient;

_____ lines without _____
6. (his / clean / long)   7. (extra / much)

ornamentation, done in _____ fabrics, obviously
8. (expensive / fine / silk)

recalled _____ paintings. He translated
9. (Japanese / old / some)

_____ ideas into _____
10. (classic / simple / these)   11. (elegant / business)

suits and gave them _____ touch. Another
12. (soft / a / feminine)

designer, Louis Darrieux, had apparently visited Tahiti, as evidenced by

_____ outfits, which bring to mind images of
13. (brightly-colored / his / wild)

_____ islands and which are perfect for
14. (far-off / tropical / South Sea)

_____ wear. But inspiration for
15. (casual / daytime)

_____ clothes came from Mexico, in Guillermo
16. (liveliest / new / the)

Pérez's collection. _____ hues combined with
17. (pink / hot / those)

_____ colors woven together with turquoise and
18. (purple / brilliant / several)

orange in _____ skirts were the sensation of
19. (cotton / long / flowing)

the show.

It has been a long time since we have seen such beautiful styles from

_____ designer; we are pleased as punch to have
20. (well-known / any / clothes)

_____ artists among us.
21. (new / fabulous / these)

2. Using Noun Modifiers

Complete the following passage by turning the phrases listed into noun modifier constructions and writing them in the appropriate blanks.

cats that live in the house	gardens where flowers grow	tea made of blackberries
dreams of childhood	trees that grow apples	a sister who is a baby
horses used for work	gardens where vegetables grow	guests staying at the house
memories of childhood	a pie made of peaches	a night in the summer
horses displayed in shows	jam made of strawberries	a house for guests to stay in
	a table in the kitchen	

My happiest memories are of visiting my grandparents' farm every summer when I was a child.

There they had many _____*apple trees*_____ that I used to climb to pick the apples. They had
1.

both _____, where roses and violets grew, and _____,
2.   3.

from which we gathered the carrots and beans that we ate at dinner.

There were some horses— _____, which helped my grandfather and
4.

the men in the fields, and even a few _____, which won prizes in the state fairs.
5.

There were a lot of cats, but they weren't _____; they roamed outside, particularly
6.

in the barn area, hunting the mice.

Sometimes my grandparents had _____, who would usually stay in the
7.

small _____ near the barn. Having these other people was fun, but I liked it even
8.

better when it was just our small family.

When we were alone, my grandmother used to make her own jellies and jams; I loved to pick

(continued on next page)

the strawberries in the fields to make my contribution to her special _____. She
9.

also made a delicious tea from the wild blackberries growing nearby. I would have that wonderful

_____ at night, along with a piece of _____ that she made
10.   11.

from her own home-grown peaches. We would sit at the _____ after clearing off
12.

the dinner dishes and talk about life, about her _____ of so many years earlier
13.

and about my _____ for the future.
14.

    Then she would gently lead me to the small, cozy bedroom that I shared with my

_____, who was too young then to appreciate the beautiful times with my
15.

grandmother. I slept soundly and peacefully every _____ that I spent at my
16.

grandmother's house and dreamed almost every night in the intervening winters that I was basking in

the warmth of her love.

3.   Forming Compound Modifiers

Following is a list of items recently purchased at Joseph and Lillian's Antique Shop.
Rewrite each item as a noun with modifiers including a compound modifier.

Joseph and Lillian's Antique Shop

1.   2 silver candlesticks   ninety-five years old
         Two ninety-five-year-old silver candlesticks

2.   1 dining room table   200 years old

        _____

3.   8 dining room chairs   covered in velvet

        _____

4.   2 Tiffany lamps   century old

        _____

5.   1 samovar   plated in silver

        _____

6.   1 chandelier   leaded with crystal

        _____

7.	2 rocking chairs	150 years old
8.	1 Persian carpet	woven by hand
9.	1 manuscript	written by hand
10.	3 coffee tables	inlaid with ivory
11.	4 serving dishes	painted by hand
12.	2 mahogany beds	carved by hand
13.	2 vases	130 years old/inlaid with gold

4. Editing

Read the following passage about a writer's first days in New York. Find and correct the sixteen errors in the modification of nouns.

Moving from the ~~country fresh~~ *fresh country* air to the head-clogging, polluted stuff they still call air presents a shock to the body. Having miraculously obtained a paying job in the, to me, publishing glamorous world, I moved with my wife and two daughters from southwest beautiful Montana with its blue, clear skies to New York, where there appeared to us to be no skies at all, only gray, dirty smog.

Within a week, my wife and children came down with a respiratory mysterious ailment. Coughing and sneezing, with eyes and nose dripping, they suffered noisily for ten days. A ten-days siege in a cramped four-rooms apartment felt like being imprisoned in a dreary, jail, cement cell. Just as the three of them were recovering from the insult to the body and soul, I succumbed to it. After only

(continued on next page)

two weeks at my new prized job, I had to call in sick. And was I sick! My forty-two-years-old, feverish body ached as it never had before. Iron gigantic hammers pounded in my head. My lungs felt like black lead, huge weights. I coughed constantly, so that I never had more than a two-hours rest, even though I took double the recommended dose of the over-the-counter cough medication we had bought at a corner drug store. Finally, after ten days, I too, recovered physically, although not psychologically, from my New York unspeakably rude reception. My three first weeks in the Big Apple gave me the feeling that I lived in a foreign and hostile country—and I still live there.

5. Personalization

Can you write vivid descriptions of people, places, or things? Choose one of the topics below, and write a few sentences about two or more people, places, or things. Use as many of the types of modifiers in the box as you can.

Determiners (**a, an, the, this, those, my,** etc.)

Sequence words (**first, second, next, last,** etc.)

Quantifiers (**one, two, few, little, many, some,** etc.)

Adjectives (of opinion; qualities; size, height, length; age; temperature; shape; color; nationalities, origins)

Nouns

TOPICS

1. Your mother and father

2. Your brothers and/or sisters

3. Your best friends

4. Your two favorite places

5. Your favorite foods

6. Two things in your house that you like a lot

7. Clothes you wear to feel comfortable, and clothes you wear to be elegant

1. Identifying Quantifiers

The following passage is from the International Almanac for the years 2000–2001. Underline the twenty-five quantifiers.

THE International Almanac
FOR
2000-2001

From November through March, <u>a lot of</u> warmer-than-usual weather is expected in the Northern Hemisphere, although not in every area. Certain parts of Europe—especially the British Isles and France—will be warm, but some parts of North America—notably western Canada and Alaska—will be somewhat colder. In western Africa, the weather will be cooler than usual, and with less rain; this is good news for people in the Caribbean and the eastern seaboard of the United States, as these conditions will probably lead to fewer hurricanes than usual in those areas. However, in Africa itself, the condition of too little precipitation will continue, and there probably won't be enough rain to produce all the crops necessary to feed the population. Elsewhere in the Southern Hemisphere, a beautiful spring and summer are predicted in South America. No tidal waves are expected this year in Australia or Japan, nor are other weather problems expected in either place.

From April through October, we will have more warm weather in a few parts of Europe, but on most of the Continent, temperatures will remain close to normal. There won't be much snow in the Alps before the end of October; after that plenty of snow is expected and should ensure a successful ski season. The amount of snow in the Andes will be normal, as will the temperatures throughout the rest of South America. In North America, the waters of the Mississippi will be high, due to a great deal of rain; we can expect two floods, neither of which will be as serious as the floods of the summer of 1993. A number of earthquakes are expected to occur during this period in Asia, but none of them will be major.

The levels of both the Atlantic and the Pacific oceans will remain the same, even though over the long term each of them is expected to rise. The hole in the ozone layer over Antarctica is expected to become slightly larger, thus permitting more harmful ultraviolet rays into the atmosphere. By this time next year, however, the news about the ozone layer may be better because of the efforts, many of which are proving successful, to control the greenhouse effect.

2. Using Quantifiers

Complete the following letter by selecting the correct quantifiers.

Dear Marco,

Well, you certainly seem to be having ___*a lot of*___ fun the United States now. I
1. (a lot of / many)

see that having _____ friends in your life makes _____ difference to
2. (a few / a little)   3. (a number of / a great deal of)

your state of mind. You should send _____ news about the lady you wrote
4. (a little / a few)

about. Is she special, or do you have _____ girlfriends? You never used to have
5. (many / much)

_____ girlfriends at all, Marco. What happened? Did you have _____
6. (any / no)   7. (a couple of / a bit of)

luck suddenly? Did you suddenly get handsome? Are _____ the girls calling you
8. (a great deal of / all)

up every day? If I sound jealous, I am. _____ weeks ago you were complaining
9. (A little / A couple of)

that _____ person you had met was ignoring you; now it seems that you have
10. (either / every)

_____ friends and that you are even doing well in_____ your
11. (an amount of / a bunch of)   12. (a couple of / a little of)

classes. I, on the other hand, may fail _____ my classes. Besides that, I lost
13. (a great deal of / most of)

_____ money last month when I invested in a "get-rich-quick" scheme. I
14. (a great many / a lot of)

borrowed money from everybody, and now I owe _____ money to
15. (many / a great deal of)

_____ our friends. Marco, do you think that you could lend me
16. (a bit of / a few of)

_____ money? I'll pay you back soon.
17. (a few / a little)

Your friend,

Ricardo

3. Using Quantifiers

Complete the selection by choosing quantifiers.

There are _____ *fewer* _____ monkeys and apes living now than previously as their habitats
1. (few / fewer / less)

are being destroyed by various human activities. There is _____ habitable land than
2. (fewer / less / few)

there used to be because of extensive development by humans.

_____ species of monkeys are in imminent danger of becoming extinct because
3. (Many / Much / A lot)

of _____ habitat loss. _____ areas in the rain forests of South America,
4. (any / many / a great deal of)   5. (Many / Much / A great deal of)

Asia, and Africa have been totally destroyed, jeopardizing the survival of _____ species.
6. (some / some of / any)

International laws now place _____ animals on lists of endangered species. While such
7. (many / much / every)

laws protect individual animals to some extent, they have not prevented habitat destruction.

Because of protective laws, _____ species of monkeys or apes are used for
8. (some / few / a few)

commercial purposes any longer. There is one kind of monkey, however, the rhesus monkey, that

has been used in _____ medical and psychological research during recent
9. (a lot of / many / a great many)

decades. Although _____ rhesus monkeys remain in their natural habitat,
10. (some / any / a little)

_____ these monkeys are also raised in captivity now for research needs.
11. (a great amount of / a great deal of / a great number of)

4. Using Quantifiers

Read the information and complete it by choosing the appropriate quantifiers.

Almost _____ *every* _____ adult in the United States has been invited to use a credit card
1. (every / either / all)

at _____ time. Usually an "invitation" to use one comes in the mail, along with a
2. (some / any / each)

_____ of flattering remarks about the exclusivity of the people chosen to use the card.
3. (great amount / number / great deal)

The temptation to take out the credit card is strong, especially among _____
4. (certain / a certain / every)

people who are not highly creditworthy at the time they receive the offer, such as students or recent

graduates. The prospect of having _____ desirable goods so easily attainable with a
5. (much of / much / many)

little plastic card can be extremely seductive.

_____ cards are issued by individual stores and are good only for purchases
6. (An amount of / Much / Some)

within the store. Others are issued by banks, through MasterCard or VISA, for example, and still others by the credit card companies themselves, such as American Express and Diners Club.

_____ oil companies and telephone companies, too, issue cards to large numbers
7. (Either of the / Any of the / Some)

of users.

_____ the credit cards work the same way. The consumer makes purchases
8. (Most of / Much of / A great deal of)

and receives bills in the mail within a month. What he or she doesn't pay that month is subject to

interest, often at a rate as high as 18 percent. Large stores and services usually have systems set up to

bill the customer directly. The bank cards work somewhat differently. When a customer uses the card

to purchase an item, the credit card issuer pays the store but deducts _____ money
9. (an amount of / a number of / a few)

from this payment as a service charge. The credit card issuer therefore profits from service charges

and from interest charges and, in most cases, also profits from an annual fee charged to the consumer

for the privilege of using the card.

_____ way, paying the store directly or paying the credit card company, if the
10. (Neither / Both / Either)

customer doesn't pay within _____ time, he or she must pay interest. Of course, the
11. (a certain / certain / little)

more he or she pays at once, the _____ interest the customer will have to pay in total.
12. (fewer / little / less)

5.　Editing

Read the following first draft of a letter from an investment counseling service.
Find and correct the thirteen errors in the use of quantifiers. (In each case,
change the quantifier; do not change other words.)

Smith & Fitch

Dear Investor:

    We know that you are a financially responsible citizen who doesn't have ~~no~~ *any* time to study

the financial markets or enough expertise to carry out sophisticated financial dealings. A few

people these days can keep up with financial developments. Because people can't keep up, we at

Smith and Fitch Investing Service are here to provide investment counseling for you.

(continued on next page)

Right now you are probably overwhelmed by having to think about the short-term and long-term needs of your family, that is, either their immediate needs and their future needs. Let us offer you a financial plan to keep you on top of your expenses and in control of your life so that you will have fewer anxiety and many more money.

We will create a portfolio for you that includes every of your assets. We will provide you with the number of information you need to make your financial decisions and several advice that comes from almost eight decades of experience. We are fully aware of each of the news that will impact your investments and can act promptly not only to preserve your capital but also to put it to the most advantageous use.

Of course, you should be diversified in your investments. We will make sure your portfolio has the right mix of stocks and bonds. You can even work with a few stock options that will earn you a few extra money. At your age, you could do very well with an annuity or a life insurance policy; neither of those will preserve your capital very safely. There are a great deal of possible scenarios; we want to develop the one that is best for you personally. We will give your situation a great number of thought and will always be available for consultation.

Please call us soon to set up an appointment.

Very truly yours,

Fred Fitch

Smith & Fitch

6. Personalization

If you win the lottery, what will you do with the money? Write some of your ideas. Include some of the phrases in the box.

First, I will pay all . . .

Then I will put a little . . .

I will invest in some . . .

I will take a few . . .

I will buy many . . .

I might buy a couple of . . .

I will contribute to certain . . .

I will finally have enough . . .

I will give some . . .

I will relax and have a lot of . . .

The Passive: Review and Expansion ▼

1. Identifying Passive Constructions

Read this letter from a young woman to her mother, written in 1898. Underline all passive constructions.

Dear Mama,

I am really excited about decorating our new home. Henry and I have consulted the best home furnishings and design experts in the city, and we <u>are being advised</u> about how and why to do everything.

First, our parlor. All our furniture will be covered in the best textiles. We'll have a gentleman's chair and a lady's chair. As you know, the gentleman's chair is designed for the comfort of the master of the house; it has arms, and the gentleman can recline comfortably. My chair is smaller because my voluminous skirts have to be accommodated, and its straight back makes me sit up straight. Our bric-a-brac and collection of miniatures must be displayed prominently, so we are having a special display cabinet built. In the dining room, the fabrics will be of leather, not luxurious textiles, because food odors can be absorbed by those heavy fabrics.

And, speaking of food, my kitchen is going to be equipped with all the latest appliances. Cooking and cleaning will be easy, with my new wood-burning stove and modern cast-iron tubs in which to have the dishes washed. An attractive kitchen helps to ensure that the meals will get served promptly and the household will be smoothly run.

Less attention has been given to the upstairs so far. Our bedroom should not be as ornate as the parlor or dining room; that would be in bad taste, and furthermore, the sleeping room is rarely seen by anyone outside the immediate family. We will certainly have the bedroom furnished with rugs instead of carpets so that they may be cleaned thoroughly each week. We have been advised to use paint rather than wallpaper in the bedroom, because stale air can be trapped in the wallpaper. We are also planning to have a modern bathroom installed, with an indoor toilet and running water.

Mama, in the end a lot of money will have been spent on the house, but I am sure it will be worth it. Oh, Mama, I can't wait until we have moved in and you come to visit us.

Your loving daughter,

Elizabeth

2. Using Active and Passive Constructions

*Complete the following information from travel brochures by putting the verbs in parentheses into either active or passive constructions. Use a form of **be** in the passive constructions.*

～～～～ Travel, Inc. ～～～～

CANCUN

Here, amid the ruins of the ancient Mayas, you _____*will find*_____ the world's most beautiful
1. (will / find)

beaches and clear blue waters. You _____ by the gentle breezes as you
2. (will / caress)

_____ languidly around the pool or on the white sand. At night, after you
3. (laze)

_____ the sensuous Yucatán cuisine, you _____ by the strolling
4. (savor)   5. (will / thrill)

Mariachi musicians.

PUERTO RICO

Experience the pleasures of Puerto Rico. Cruise the crystal-clear waters of the Atlantic,

dive into the Caribbean and enjoy fishing and nighttime swimming. The galleries and shops of

cobblestoned Old San Juan _____, and its restaurants _____.
6. (must / see)   7. (must / enjoy)

Both Spanish and English _____ here.
8. (speak)

HAWAII

You _____ by the astonishing array of luxurious tropical products, from sun-
9. (will / delight)

ripened papayas to macadamia nuts and orchids. Hawaii _____ long ago
10. (settle)

by Polynesians, who _____ by the beauty and lushness of the islands and
11. (enchant)

therefore never _____ them. You won't want to leave either!
12. (leave)

JAMAICA

Here in the land of luxurious vegetation, cool mountains, and gorgeous beaches, you

_____ the original reggae and calypso music. Dance to the steel bands, and enjoy
13. (can / experience)

the beautiful weather, the waterfalls, and the hospitality of people who _____
14. (speak)

(continued on next page)

a special elegant English. In this romantic spot in the Caribbean, you _____
15. (will / enchant)

by everything around you.

BERMUDA

This perfect gem in the Atlantic, which _____ by England, retains its British
16. (colonize)

traditions and is considered the most quietly charming island in the Western Hemisphere.

Automobiles _____ in much of Bermuda; bicycles and motor scooters
17. (allow / not)

_____ at reasonable prices. There are many excellent shopping opportunities,
18. (may / rent)

especially for articles that _____ from the United Kingdom.
19. (import)

3. Using Passive Constrtuctions

*Read this letter from a young woman to her mother, written in 2025. Complete
the letter with passive constructions with* **be** *and the indicated verbs. Some
items may have additional correct answers.*

HI, MOM,

KEVIN AND I ARE EXCITED ABOUT OUR NEW HOUSE, WHICH _*is being constructed*_
1. (construct)

AS I WRITE THIS LETTER. CONSTRUCTION _____ BY THE ASSEMBLERS ON
2. (begin)

MONDAY AND SHOULD BE FINISHED BY NEXT MONDAY. AS YOU KNOW, THE HOUSE

_____ BY COMPUTER LAST WEEK.
3. (completely / design)

THE HOUSE IS ROUND, AND EACH OF THE ROOMS IS SHAPED LIKE A PIECE OF PIE. THE

MAIN LIVING AREA, WHICH IS UPSTAIRS, _____ BY PRICELESS VIEWS OF
4. (surround)

THE OUTDOORS. THROUGH GLASS DOORS WE CAN SEE THE LAKE, AND WE ARE NOT GOING TO LET

THIS VIEW _____ BY OUTSIDE WALLS OR LARGE ELECTRONIC EQUIPMENT.
5. (spoil)

DOWNSTAIRS, NEAR WHERE THE MEDIA AND COMMUNICATIONS ROOMS _____,
6. (be / build)

WE WILL ALSO _____ SO WE CAN _____ BY A
7. (have / a garden center / put in)   8. (have / organic vegetables / grow)

GARDENER. ALL THE WALLS, FLOORS, AND CEILINGS ARE MADE OF BEAUTIFUL

PASTEL-COLORED STEEL, SO THAT EVERYTHING _____ VERY EASILY
9. (can / clean)

BY JUST PUSHING THE BUTTONS ON OUR SUCTION VACUUM. THE FURNITURE, TOO,

_____ BECAUSE THE UPHOLSTERY, WHICH IS MADE OF PAPER THAT LOOKS
10. (can / easily / maintain)

LIKE OLD-FASHIONED COTTON OR LINEN, _____ EVERY WEEK. I WOULD
11. (can / replace)

LIKE SOME TWENTIETH-CENTURY PAINTINGS FOR OUR WALLS, BUT KEVIN PREFERS THE WORK

OF YOUNG PAINTERS WHO _____ BY THE IDEAS OF THE TWENTY-FIRST
12. (have / influence)

CENTURY.

THIS IS OUR FIRST HOUSE, AND THE MONEY THAT WE HAVE _____
13. (have to / budget)

CAREFULLY. OUR MONEY _____ WISELY, AND EVERY PURCHASE
14. (must / spend)

_____. WE ARE GOING TO _____ TO LAST A LONG TIME.
15. (must / carefully / consider)   16. (have / everything / make)

I LOVE EVERYTHING THAT _____ SO FAR. I CAN'T WAIT UNTIL NEXT
17. (have / do)

WEEK, WHEN THE CONSTRUCTION _____ AND OUR NEW FURNITURE AND
18. (will / have / complete)

EQUIPMENT _____. AND, OF COURSE, I CAN'T WAIT UNTIL YOU COME
19. (will / have / install)

VISIT US IN OUR NEW HOME.

LOVE,

YOUR DAUGHTER RENU

4.   Recognizing and Writing Passive Causatives with *Have*

"Action Line" is a newspaper column that helps readers who have specific problems.
Underline passive causatives in readers' letters to "Action Line." (Each letter has
one or more causatives.) Then complete the responses from "Action Line," by
changing the phrase in parentheses into a passive causative with **have**.

1. My grandparents have lived in their apartment building for nearly 30 years. Now they have termites, and

the landlord is refusing to <u>have the building treated</u> by professional exterminators. He says that he can't

afford it, so he's just having their apartment sprayed. I know that's not enough. What can be done?

Solution: Action Line did it. We called the Department of Business Regulations, which handles

complaints like yours, and they _*have already had the landlord investigated*_.
(have / already / investigate the landlord)

If the landlord doesn't properly get rid of the termites by the 15th of next month, he will

be fined $1,000.

(continued on next page)

2. I have a Picky eight-track tape player. It used to work fine, but since the last snowstorm, it's been making a lot of noise. My nephew asked me if I had ever had the heads of the tape player cleaned. I said no. Is that what I should do? I have so many tapes I would like to hear clearly.

Solution: Les Garth, owner of The Audio Place, told Action Line that he doesn't recommend cleaning the heads of tape players like yours. He said you

_____, which he can do for you for $7.95 each.
(should / transfer the tapes to regular cassettes)

3. I had some furniture sent to my house from Modella Furniture Company in North Carolina. The furniture arrived, but a leg on one of the chairs had broken off. I wrote to the company and spoke to a secretary there on the phone, but it has been two months now and nothing has been done. What can you do, Action Line?

Solution: Action Line was able to get through to the president of the company. We arranged to

_____, and Modella has agreed to pay for a
(an insurance adjuster look at your table)

replacement table if necessary.

4. I took my new, very expensive formal gown to Alfie's Alterations to have it shortened. It was shortened, all right! When I got it back, the skirt was five inches above my knees! Alfie's apologized and gave me credit to have future alterations done there, but this doesn't compensate me for the hundreds of dollars I spent on the dress, which is now ruined. Action Line, can't something be done?

Solution: Yes, it already has been done. Action Line sent a representative to Alfie's. Alfie Brown, the owner, said to replace the dress and to _____.
(send the bill to him)

5. My car is 11 years old and has been running smoothly all this time. Then last month it began stalling. I have had it checked by my mechanic, and he wasn't able to fix it. I am at my wits' end, because I love this car. Any suggestions, Action Line?

Solution: Action Line has contacted the manufacturer. They tell us that an 11-year-old car is, of course, under no warranty, but since they want their customers to be happy, they said to take it to the nearest dealer, where they _____,
(will / fix the problem)

if it's at all possible.

6. Our 13-year-old son volunteers at a shelter for homeless people. This work is very important to him. The trouble is that both my wife and I work full time and we live in a rural area with inadequate public

transportation. The shelter had had a car sent for him each day but can no longer do so. Any suggestions, Action Line?

Solution: Action Line called the volunteer group Side-by-Side Rides. They pick up deserving people like your son and take them where they need to go. You can call the group at 555-0965 and arrange to _____.
(pick up your son)

5. Using Passive Constructions with *Get*

Read the following response from Marco to his friend Ricardo. Complete the letter with passive constructions with **get** *and the indicated verbs.*

Dear Ricardo,

I'm sorry to hear that you _____*got hit*_____ by money problems, although it sounds like
1. (hit)
some of them are your own fault. I'm also sorry that I won't be able to help you. I've got some

problems of my own.

Last week, I had to _____. It suddenly refused to go—right in the middle of
2. (my car/fix)
rush hour traffic! After two hours, it finally _____ by a tow truck to a repair shop.
3. (tow)
The next day my car was running fine again. But I _____ $450 for the repair.
4. (charge)
This week has been even worse. On Monday, someone broke into my apartment. All my

good things _____: my TV, my sound system, and even my new bicycle. In the middle
5. (steal)
of all this, I also _____ by Lisa, the girl I wrote you about. "Get dumped" is an
6. (dump)
expression that means she doesn't want to go out with me anymore. At least I think she doesn't.

About your situation: I think you should get a night job. You really need the money, and working

will keep you out of trouble. If you can _____ by a hotel chain, for example, you might
7. (hire)
have the beginnings of a really good managerial job later. I hear that they like to hire young people

to work at night. If the person does well, he often _____ to stay on for a real job.
8. (ask)
I think you would be great at it. All you have to do is behave yourself and make sure you don't

_____ because of doing something stupid.
9. (fire)
Hopefully, things will be better for both of us soon.

Marco

6. Changing Active Constructions to Passive Constructions

Improve the writing style in the following descriptions of ingredients used in Mexican cooking by changing the underlined sentences and clauses from active constructions to passive constructions. For each sentence where there is a change, write the full sentence, keeping the same tense and modal auxiliaries. Do not use **people** *or other indefinite words in your* **by** *phrases in your passive sentences.*

1. **Sesame seeds**   <u>People use sesame seeds in Mexican sauces.</u> <u>You can toast them easily.</u>
      a.   b.
   <u>The Spanish introduced them to Mexico</u>. And before that, <u>the Moors had brought them to Spain</u>.
                       c.   d.

   a. ___*Sesame seeds are used in Mexican sauces.*_____

   b. _____

   c. _____

   d. _____

2. **Pepitas (pumpkin seeds)**   <u>People grind pepitas for use in sauces</u>. <u>People also eat them whole.</u>
                                                a.   b.
   <u>Even if people have ground them</u>, the sauce has a rough texture. <u>People have used pepitas since</u>
                  c.   d.
   <u>pre-Columbian times</u>.

   a. _____

   b. _____

   c. _____

   d. _____

3. **Chorizo**   Chorizo is similar in appearance to a sausage. In Mexico, <u>people make it of unsmoked</u>
                                                                                          a.
   <u>meat and spices</u>. In Spain <u>people smoke the meat</u>.
                                        b.

   a. _____

   b. _____

4. **Jicama**   Jicama is a brown-skinned root vegetable with a white, crisp flesh similar to that of a
   radish. Street vendors in Mexico sell jicama in thick slices <u>that somebody has sprinkled with salt,</u>
                                                                                a.
   <u>lime juice, and chili powder</u>.

   a. _____

5. **Avocados**   <u>People consider avocados a true delicacy</u>. If they are hard, <u>somebody should allow</u>
                                  a.   b.
   <u>them to ripen</u>. <u>People make guacamole from avocados</u>. <u>People also use avocados in salads</u>
                                      c.   d.
   <u>and as garnish</u>.

a. _____

b. _____

c. _____

d. _____

6. ***Banana leaves***   People steam meat in little packets of banana leaves. First, <u>you must soften</u>
a.   b.

<u>them over a flame</u>. Then, <u>you wrap the meat and other ingredients in them</u>.
c.

a. _____

b. _____

c. _____

7. ***Plantains***   These look like bananas but are larger and firmer. <u>People cook them in various ways</u>,
a.

including deep-frying and baking. <u>You may substitute firm green bananas</u>.
b.

a. _____

b . _____

8. ***Tortillas***   These are round and look like pancakes. <u>People can eat them with any meal</u>.
a.

<u>People make them from corn or wheat flour</u>. <u>People can now find frozen tortillas in supermarkets</u>.
b.   c.

a. _____

b. _____

c. _____

9. ***Chilies***   <u>People use chilies to season many different dishes</u>. There are various kinds of chilies. In
a.

degree of spiciness, they range from mild to very hot. <u>Humans have consumed chili-seasoned foods</u>
b.

<u>for more than 8,000 years</u>.

a. _____

b. _____

10. ***Corn***   <u>People use corn widely in Mexico</u>. In Mexican cooking, <u>people waste no part of the corn</u>.
a.   b.

<u>People use the ears, husks, silk, and kernels in different ways</u>. This was the first plant <u>that people</u>
c.   d.

<u>cultivated in Mexico</u>. Archaeologists found evidence that dates it to 5000 B.C.

a. _____

b. _____

c. _____

d. _____

7. Editing

Read the following student paper. Find and correct the ten errors in the use of passives.

        explained
A famous mystery that has never been really ~~explain~~ is that of the Devil's Triangle, which also known as the Bermuda Triangle. These names refer to an area in the Atlantic Ocean where, over a period of centuries, many mysterious disappearances of ships and airplanes have been occurred. A satisfactory explanation of the disappearances has never found. While many theories about turbulence and other atmospheric disturbances have been proposing, no meteorologic peculiarities about the area have proven. Violent storms and downward air currents have frequently been record there, but nothing has been find outside the limits of real and possible weather conditions.

        Boundaries of the triangle usually are form by drawing an imaginary line from Melbourne, Florida, to Bermuda to Puerto Rico and back to Florida. However, larger boundaries draw by some writers who want to treat far-ranging disappearances as part of the Bermuda Triangle mystery.

8. Personalization

What person outside your family has played an important part in your life? Write something about how this person has influenced you. Include some of the phrases in the box.

> I have been most influenced by . . .
>
> I was helped by _____ to . . .
>
> I was persuaded by _____ to . . .
>
> I was taught by _____ to . . .
>
> My values were formed because . . .
>
> I am still inspired by _____ , especially by the way he/she . . .
>
> His/Her influence can be seen in . . .
>
> _____ will always be remembered by me for . . .

U N I T

9

Reporting
Ideas and Facts
with Passives

▼

1. **Identifying Passive Constructions**

Read this magazine article. Underline the passive constructions which report ideas and facts.

STAY WELL MAGAZINE

It <u>used to be thought</u> that people caught colds by sitting in drafts, going out in cold weather, or going from hot to cold temperatures quickly. But now these ideas are believed to be false. It is now known that colds spread only by viruses transmitted from one person to another. Surprisingly, it is not the fact of being near an infected person that causes another person to catch a cold; it is now understood that transmission of viruses occurs most frequently when healthy people touch an object that the infected person has recently touched, such as a doorknob or a telephone, and then touch their own noses or mouths without having washed their hands well.

Colds are regarded as bothersome, but often unavoidable. Most of the time, the symptoms—a sore throat, runny nose, sneezing, mild cough, and headache—run their course and disappear within a week, with or without treatment. Antibiotics are assumed to be of no use whatsoever in combating a cold.

Chicken soup has been found to help relieve the symptoms of a cold by opening up the breathing passages and relieving the congestion. For many years, the power of chicken soup had been considered just an old wives' tale, but recently scientific research was reported in the *New England Journal of Medicine* showing that the custom of taking chicken soup for a cold actually is effective in relieving its symptoms.

For treatment of a cold, then, it is recommended that a person ease his or her symptoms by drinking plenty of fluids, especially hot fluids, and getting extra rest. To alleviate the general discomfort medically, aspirin and ibuprofen are known to help; to ease the congestion and runny nose, antihistamines and decongestants are suggested.

As the old saying goes, an ounce of prevention is worth a pound of cure. That is, measures to avoid catching the cold virus are considered more effective than measures to get rid of it.

2.　Using Passives to Report Ideas

Read the following conversation between Dr. Carl Clark, the host of a radio talk show, "Raising the Modern Child," and Margaret, a grandparent who is calling the show for advice. Complete the blanks with passive constructions, using the indicated verbs in a correct tense.

Caller: I used to hear the saying that "children should be seen not heard." I was brought up that way and tried to bring up my children that way. Now I see my daughter permitting her children to do almost anything they want. Isn't this kind of permissiveness bad?

Dr. Clark: The idea that children should be seen and not heard ___*used to be considered*___ one of
1. (used to / consider)

the basic principles for raising children. However, in the modern world, this idea

_____ to have made much trouble by causing neurosis in children. It
2. (believe)

_____ that by making children behave quietly, stifling all their
3. (previously / think)

feelings, and just keeping them pretty to look at, the children would grow up to be

polite, law-abiding citizens. While this is true to a large extent in many cases, now it

_____ that imposing too many restrictions will inhibit the child too
4. (understand)

much and can cause serious mental problems.

Caller: But, Carl, doesn't letting a child always have his or her own way spoil the child?

Dr. Clark: Of course, not setting limits on a child's behavior is not good training. But, it

_____ that constantly thwarting children, and not permitting them to
5. (well / know)

express their feelings can lead to serious frustration and possibly non-productive or

antisocial behavior patterns. The trick is to lead children strongly and correct them gently.

Caller: I really can't agree with you, Doctor. I believe that if you spare the rod, you spoil the child.

Children need punishment.

Dr. Clark: You _____ by many as correct, Margaret. But let me warn you: It
6. (would / perceive)

_____ by all child-rearing experts these days that you MUST spare
7. (widely / confirm)

the rod. At the same time, you should not spoil the child. It _____
8. (have / well / establish)

for quite some time now that children must be able to express themselves, but they must

be taught to do so in a socially acceptable way.

(continued on next page)

Caller: Well, Carl, you _____ by everyone to be the big expert, but I am
9. (know)

sorry, I just disagree with what you're telling me.

Dr. Clark: Well, Margaret, for many years now my kind of thinking _____ to be
10. (consider)

correct. You are entitled to have your opinion. But don't worry about your grandchildren.

What your daughter is doing _____ to be the right thing.
11. (can / assume)

3. Using Passives to Report Ideas

*Read the following article. Complete the blanks with passive constructions, using
the indicated verbs.*

Until recently, backgammon ___*was regarded*___ in America as an exotic, unfamiliar game.
1. (regard)

Today, backgammon _____ to be the fastest-growing game in popularity, and it
2. (believe)

_____ to have millions of dedicated players, hundreds of clubs, and an international
3. (claim)

circuit of major tournaments. Backgammon experts _____ to command lesson fees of
4. (report)

over $150 per hour now.

How old is backgammon? Historians are not sure. It _____ exactly when the
5. (not / know)

game originated, but when archaeologists excavated the ancient Sumerian city of Ur, they found in the

royal cemetery five game boards that closely resembled early backgammon boards; from this, it

_____ that the game existed five thousand years ago. Similar to the game boards
6. (now / assume)

unearthed at Ur was a board discovered among the treasures in the tomb of the Egyptian king

Tutankhamen, from around 1500 B.C. Backgammon _____ to have been popular among
7. (also / think)

the common Egyptians, because ancient Egyptian wall paintings show people playing a table game.

Oddly enough, the Spanish explorer Francisco Pizarro in the early sixteenth century described

the Aztecs in Mexico playing a game remarkably like the Egyptians' game. After this similarity had

been established, it _____ that the early people of the Americas might have migrated
8. (conjecture)

to the Western Hemisphere from areas near Egypt.

The ancient Greeks and Romans, too, _____ to have played a game like
9. (now / believe)

backgammon. Plato commented on its popularity, and it _____ by those who study
10. (say)

ancient Greece that he might have played it himself. It _____ that *tabulae,* a Roman

11. (know)

version of the game, was popular in Pompeii, because a *tabulae* board was found in the courtyard of

almost every villa in the ruins there.

We know quite a bit about backgammon in the eighteenth century. For example, backgammon

_____ to have been popular among clergymen and physicians in Europe, and in

12. (know)

America, Thomas Jefferson _____ by some scholars to have played it for relaxation

13. (now / think)

during the time when he was writing the Declaration of Independence.

Backgammon's popularity has risen and fallen though the ages. It _____ that its

14. (can / safely / assume)

popularity will fall and rise again.*

* Based on Richard B. Manchester, *Amazing Facts,* (New York: Bristol Park Books, 1991).

4. Editing

*Read the following first draft of an article. Find and correct the twenty-four
errors in the forms of passives to report ideas, and other passives.*

> *declared*
> In Washington yesterday, it was ~~declaring~~ by an advisory panel to the Senate
>
> that nicotine is definitely an addictive drug. This formal declaration believes to go
>
> further than any previous one in officially condemning the use of tobacco, and it
>
> may be the first step towards government regulation of tobacco distribution.
>
> For many years now, the dangers of cigarettes been recognized. It is no
>
> longer consider sophisticated to smoke, and in fact, people who do so are now
>
> considering unwise. More and more, smoking in public places has eliminated by
>
> local and state laws. Smoking now prohibited in many places: in hospitals, in
>
> government buildings, in business offices, and on domestic flights. While gigantic
>
> strides have made in the war against smoking, among serious non-smokers it is still
>
> thinking that enough hasn't been doing yet. These non-smokers believe that almost
>
> all smoking should be illegal, even in some private homes. Smoking in areas where

(continued on next page)

there are children is considering by them to be a form of child abuse. In addition, precisely because of the addictive qualities of tobacco, they want to eliminate children's access to it.

Not everyone shares these beliefs. Although it has now been establishing that the effects of smoking are in fact disastrous, it also know that many citizens deeply resent being told what to do. It feels by militant smokers that the government might be able to exert too much control over people's lives by having the ability to legislate the use of tobacco. If any laws to restrict smoking further are going to be proposed, it is assumes that the militant smokers will fight hard against them.

In addition, the problems of enforcing the no-smoking laws are regard as very difficult. Very few violators fined, and even fewer jailed. Understandably, the police don't want to spend their time apprehending an illegal smoker when three blocks away a robbery may be taking place and a police officer will need.

The antismokers have become optimistic, however. A public awareness about the evils of smoking now exists, and smoking not permitted in many places anymore. Programs and clinics have established all over to help people stop smoking. Children are being educating to be aware of the dangers of smoking. It is conjecturing that by the year 2010, smoking will been almost eliminated.

5. Personalization

What strange often-told stories have you heard of? Do you know mysteries like that of the Bermuda Triangle? Stories of supernatural creatures such as witches, vampires, and ghosts? Superstitions about things that bring bad luck or things that bring good luck? Write a paragraph about what people say about a mystery, a supernatural creature, or several superstitions. Include some of the phrases in the box.

It is said that . . .	. . . are said to . . .
It is thought that . . .	. . . are thought to . . .
It is believed that . . .	. . . are believed to . . .
It is claimed that . . .	. . . are claimed to . . .

_____

_____

_____

_____

_____

_____

_____

_____

_____

_____

_____

_____

_____

_____

_____

_____

_____

UNIT

10

Gerunds

1. Identifying Gerunds

Read this brochure for a health club. Underline all the gerunds. Do not underline present participles or the continuous forms of the verbs.

WELCOME TO THE SUPER SPARTAN SPA

Exercising increases energy and is also an important factor in relieving stress. You will find that you have more energy and feel less stress after you have been exercising here for a few days. Even if you have been inactive in the past that won't keep you from building your physical capability through training. Here at the Super Spartan Spa, you can shape up very quickly by participating in the activities most appropriate for you. Brisk, regular, and sustained activities, such as fast walking, jogging, or swimming, will improve the efficiency of your heart and lungs. Your flexibility and muscle strength will be improved by lifting weights or doing gymnastics.

Are you avoiding exercise because you don't have anyone to exercise with? Many people don't enjoy exercising alone.

Here at the Super Spartan Spa you will find hiking, cycling, tennis, and other activities that provide opportunities for socializing. Being included in groups that have specific objectives, such as bicycling 50 miles in one day, will benefit you socially as well as physically. You will find our exercise program interesting and involving.

Exercise stimulates the pituitary gland to produce endorphins, substances that affect mood, perception of pain, memory retention, and learning. Producing these endorphins is the body's way of alleviating feelings of depression and stress. Thus, strenuous and focused exercise can even be extremely helpful in improving your outlook on life.

ENJOY THE SUPER SPARTAN SPA!

2. Using the Perfect Form of Gerunds

Read this police report on a witness questioned about a robbery. Fill in the blanks by making gerunds in the perfect form from the verbs given.

Officers Brody and Méndez investigated a robbery that occurred on the night of June 23, at 10 Seacoast Terrace, the home of John and Jane Butler. They questioned Mark Abbott, a family friend and possible suspect. Abbott denied ____*having visited*____ the Butler house on the night of the robbery. In fact, he regretted
1. (visit)

_____ there, saying that if he had been, the robbery would never have
2. (not / be)

happened. He admitted _____ there earlier that day. He couldn't recall
3. (stop by)

_____ anything suspicious at the house. Nor could he remember
4. (see)

_____ anyone near the house. He mentioned _____ the
5. (meet)   6. (telephone)

house that evening, but he said that nobody had answered. Abbott acknowledged

_____ suspicious at that point, since the Butlers had said they would
7. (become)

definitely be at home. However; he explained his that _____ by to
8. (not / stop)

check the house was because of the lateness of the hour. Officers Brody and

Méndez then excused him, believing that he did not commit the robbery.

3. Using the Passive Form of Gerunds

*Complete the following article by filling in the blanks with the passive form of gerunds made from the verbs given in parentheses. (Use the verb **be** in the passive gerunds.)*

Soliciting business and money by telephone has become a common practice in the United

States. The telephone calls often come during the dinner hour. But people usually don't appreciate

____*being telephoned*____ at home by strangers, especially while they are eating. They resent
1. (telephone)

_____ at that time with offers of opportunity to obtain merchandise, to contribute
2. (bother)

to a charity, or to invest money. _____ to respond politely to this kind of telephonic
3. (Require)

intrusion is too much for many people, who end up by shouting rudely or slamming down the telephone.

On the other hand, some people respond enthusiastically to the idea of _____ for
4. (have / choose)

these telephone offers. As some offers are actually frauds however, the importance of

(continued on next page)

_____ by such offers must be emphasized. For example, if a solicitor says, "Your
    5. (not / fool)

_____ to participate in this offer is a unique opportunity. You must act quickly,"
    6. (have / select)

the person should be extremely wary.

Here are some tips for dealing with telephone solicitations. Above all, you should avoid

_____ as gullible. If you want to invest money, you should know the company well; if
    7. (perceive)

not, you risk _____. As long as you don't mind _____ at home in the
              8. (cheat)   9. (disturb)

first place, take the time to ask the telephone solicitor pertinent questions. But you could also respond,

as many other people do to the annoyance of _____ by telephone too often: Just turn
                                              10. (have / solicit)

off your phone at dinnertime and enjoy a peaceful meal.

4. Using Possessives with Gerunds

Read the following letter written to Pamela's advice column. Combine each pair
of sentences, using a possessive noun or possessive pronoun and a gerund in
each new sentence you write.

Pamela's Advice

Dear Pamela:

My friend Helen married Tom last year, against my advice. They didn't know each other very well at the time, as they had met only three weeks prior to their wedding. Now they are discovering things about each other that they don't like.

For example:

1. Tom smokes cigars in the bedroom. Helen can't stand this.

    Helen can't stand Tom's smoking
    cigars in the bedroom.

2. Helen talks on the phone to her boss on weekends. Tom is annoyed by this.

    _____

    _____

3. Tom is rude to Helen's family. Helen can't tolerate this.

    _____

    _____

4. Helen's cooking is terrible. Tom dislikes this.

    _____

    _____

5. Tom swears at other drivers. Helen is disturbed by this.

    _____

    _____

6. Tom spends hours in front of the TV. Helen resents this.

    _____

    _____

7. Helen snores. Tom can't sleep because of this.

_____

_____

8. They fight all the time when I'm around them. I can't stand this.

_____

_____

9. You always have good advice. I really appreciate this.

_____

_____

So please tell me—what should Helen and Tom do?

Bothered in Boston

5. Editing

In the following passage, there are sixteen verbs that should be put into a gerund form. Find these verbs and put them into the correct gerund form.

Before the twentieth century, hobbies were something that only the wealthy had the time or money to enjoy. The present-day enthusiasm for ~~participate~~ *participating* in an absorbing activity is the result of many people's bless with greater prosperity and more free time. Some popular hobbies are as old as civilization. Play music, paint, and sculpt have always fascinated many. Collect valuable objects, rare manuscripts, and art treasures were the hobbies of rulers in ancient times. At the end of the nineteenth century, a strong interest in arts and crafts developed, and people expressed themselves in weave, pottery make, wood carve, and other artistic activities. Today, many individuals enjoy use computers or make their own movies with video cassettes.

Many sports and games are also popular hobbies. Sports such as tennis and sail provide activity and competition; so does play such games as chess and bridge. Recognize as an expert in one of these areas can give one a feeling of satisfaction. Hobbies have long provided a means for people's express themselves and find enjoyment.

6. Personalization

You have probably experienced some great changes at certain times in your life. Write a short essay about one of those changes. Include some of the phrases in the box, making sure that the phrases are followed by appropriate gerunds.

I'll never forget . . .

I don't regret . . .

I had some problems . . .

I began . . .

I finally became comfortable in my new situation by . . .

I really enjoyed . . .

For others about to do the same thing, I would recommend . . .

I am now very happy about . . .

1. Identifying Infinitives

Read the following report by a sociology student. Underline the infinitives. Include the negative **not***.*

Human beings need <u>to be loved and cared for</u>. When warm feelings exist between people, it is natural to give and receive love. In fact, a common proverb is: "It is better to give than to receive."

Children who do well in school seem to be receiving strong and consistent love and support from their families. On the other hand, many antisocial adolescents appear not to have received much tender, loving care during their childhood. In their desire to be included in a group, some teenagers are easily seduced into gangs. Often they are disappointed not to receive from other gang members the love that they had been yearning for.

After years in a gang, it is common for these young people to become hardened; it is then extremely difficult for them to be rehabilitated into society. Unfortunately, most are expected to continue on their sad and seemingly hopeless journey through life. However, some who are fortunate enough to have been reached and touched by enlightened and caring social workers do reform and become productive members of society. With guidance and help, it is possible, even for those exhibiting antisocial behaviors to be rehabilitated.

2. Using Infinitives of Purpose

Match the places in column I with the activities in column II. Then on the following page, write a sentence for each place telling the activity that would be your reason for going there. Use the example sentence as a model and include an infinitive of purpose.

I	**II**
1. Antarctica	A. photograph large wild animals
2. The Caribbean	B. shop for original designer clothes
3. Switzerland or Colorado	C. dance the samba and lambada
4. Egypt	D. sail, swim, dive, and snorkel
5. Japan	E. visit pyramids
6. Kenya	F. ski
7. Paris	G. meet Mickey Mouse and Donald Duck
8. Italy	H. observe penguins
9. Brazil	I. see Mount Fujiyama
10. Disneyland	J. walk around the ruins of ancient Rome

U N I T

11

Infinitives

(continued on next page)

75

1. _I would go to Antarctica to observe penguins._

2. _____

3. _____

4. _____

5. _____

6. _____

7. _____

8. _____

9. _____

10. _____

3. Using Infinitives

Read the following article from the society section of a newspaper. Complete the article by filling in the blanks with the infinitives of the verbs indicated. Use perfect and passive forms where they are needed.

Martha and Sam Adams celebrated their fiftieth wedding anniversary last Saturday. They were given a surprise party by sixty of their friends and relatives.

Martha said she was very lucky **to have been** at the party where she 1. (be) met Sam fifty-one years ago. She said that at that party she was very excited when Sam asked her _____, although she 2. (dance) pretended _____ nonchalant. 3. (be)

Sam said that he is extremely fortunate _____ married to Martha for 4. (be) all those years and that he believes that everybody must envy him. The Adamses both mentioned several times that they were happy _____ by their loved ones. 5. (remember) Throughout the evening they often stopped _____ about their lives together. 6. (reminisce) Martha started _____ a little 7. (cry) when the orchestra played "The Anniversary Waltz," and Sam shed a few tears, too, although he struggled _____ them. At 8. (conceal) the end of the evening, Sam and Martha swore _____ and _____ 9. (love)   10. (cherish) each other for the next fifty years and invited everybody _____ their 11. (attend) hundredth anniversary celebration.

4. Using Infinitives

Read the following page from Beth's diary. Complete the diary by filling in the blanks with the infinitives of the verbs indicated. Use perfect and passive forms where they are needed.

Dear Diary,

Today is the first anniversary of Grandpa Max's death, and I have been thinking about him all day. How fortunate I am _to have had_ a Grandpa like him. It was easy _____
1. (have)   2. (love)
him; he was always doing things that made us love him. I thought about how when we were little

he sometimes used to pretend _____ a big, growling bear—we would be so
3. (be)
delighted _____ and _____ one of his big bear hugs that we would
4. (pick up)   5. (give)
squeal with pleasure. And I remember how he taught me _____ a bicycle when I
6. (ride)
was five. I had been yearning _____ by my older cousins to ride bicycles with them,
7. (invite)
but I wasn't able to until Grandpa taught me how.

I loved it when he would come _____ us. He always brought us little gifts
8. (visit)
guaranteed _____ us laugh, like a ring that turned into a squirt gun and a cuckoo
9. (make)
clock with a Mickey Mouse inside. And when we needed someone _____ to,
10. (talk)
Grandpa was such a good listener. He would encourage us _____ stories,
11. (tell)
_____ big things, and _____ to reach bigger goals.
12. (imagine)   13. (try)
Then, when I was about eight, I remember that I was afraid _____ far from
14. (go)
home. I was afraid of ghosts, and I expected _____ by one at any moment. Grandpa
15. (attack)
persuaded me _____ down the street with him, past one more house each
16. (walk)
time we went out together, until we got to the end of the block. Then, with him, I managed

_____ two blocks away from home, then three, until finally I was able to go
17. (go)
everywhere, and I forgot about the ghosts. Years later, on my sixteenth birthday, Grandpa permitted

me _____ him around the block in his car, and I felt so proud, even though my
18. (drive)
cousin Johnny said that Grandpa must have been crazy _____ me do that.
19. (let)
When he died, I cried. I would like _____ able to tell him I loved him just one
20. (be)
more time before he died. _____ a grandpa like Grandpa Max is very sad. But I think
21. (Lose)
that never _____ Grandpa Max would have been even sadder.
22. (have)

5. Using Infinitives

Read Ricardo's reply to Marco's last letter. In each part, put in the correct form of the infinitive chosen from the verbs in the box above it. Use perfect and passive forms where they are needed.

be	do	get	give	learn	work

Dear Marco,

You sure handed out some strong advice. Well, it came to the right place. I took your

suggestion and applied for a job at a hotel. The manager offered ___*to give*___ me
                                                                        1.

a job at the front desk, starting next Monday night. He wants me _____ all
                                                                    2.

aspects of the job while working. I think I can manage _____ and study
                                                          3.

at the same time. _____ both will be difficult but necessary if I am
                     4.

_____ out of this mess. I really have no choice. _____
   5.   6.

heavily in debt is a terrible thing!

do	give	leave	show up	take

I am expected _____ for work at 5:00 p.m. I'll work until 1:00 a.m.,
                  7.

unless I don't want _____ a break. In that case, I'll be permitted
                       8.

_____ at midnight. The manager said I would be allowed _____
   9.   10.

some studying at the desk when things are slow, but I am required _____
                                                                      11.

first priority to the details of the job.

get	give	invest	take advantage of	tell	trick

I am really sorry _____ myself into such a mess. It sure was dumb.
                     12.

Sometimes I think that when brains were being given out, I was unlucky enough

_____ 13. a very small one. I don't know what I was thinking when I allowed

myself _____ 14. in the way that I was. The guy on the phone sounded so smart

when he was persuading me _____ 15. in his operation. I am really embarrassed

_____ 16., especially since now, of course, the trick seems so obvious. I'm asking

you not _____ 17. anybody about this.

| be | behave | forget | get | go out | pursue | talk | tell |

And, what about you and Lisa? If she is important to you, I hope you won't just

decide _____ 18. about her. Instead, you have to continue _____ 19.

her seriously. The problem might be the way you sometimes talk to people. Try

_____ 20. more diplomatic with Lisa than you are with me and with everyone

else. Sometimes you are so honest that girls are reluctant _____ 21. to you

about any delicate subject; they don't want _____ 22. harsh realities by you.

_____ 23. Lisa back, Marco, you have to be prepared _____ 24. much

better than you usually do. Call her and very nicely ask her _____ 25. with you.

Maybe she will. Let me know what happens.

Thanks for helping me out.

Ricardo

6. Editing

Read the following article. Find and correct the twenty-five errors in the use of infinitives. In some cases the form of the infinitive is incorrect. In other cases infinitives aren't used where they should be used or are used where they shouldn't be used. In some cases, the infinitive is correct.

    In order *to* enjoy a full life in one's later years, it is vital to maintaining close relationships and to keep physically active. To involve oneself in absorbing interests is important, as this involvement encourages a person to expanding and engage in healthy activity.

(continued on next page)

There is example after example to illustrates how rewarding life can be at an older age. For instance, an elderly widower in California has learned how to knitting, an activity that allows him not only artistic expression, but also opportunities meeting women available for to socialize with. Now he is so often invited dine at ladies' homes that he hasn't needed cook a meal in four months. In New York state, a seventy-two-year-old grandmother took up to run six years ago and last year ran all twenty-six miles of the New York Marathon. This year she expects being awarded a prize for having made the most improvement in speed within one year. A Canadian couple developed their lifelong interest in to ice skate into the most successful skating school in eastern Ontario, and they are preparing open another school near Boston. In California, a ninety-two-year-old woman who is a Scrabble champion wrote a how-to book on the subject, and she volunteers teach less-accomplished players her strategies. These and other examples serve demonstrate that a can-do attitude leads to a rewarding life. Elders should be encouraged accept realistic challenges like these.

To having regular and strenuous activities is important, even for people in their 80s and 90s. It's never too late to begin physical training. The older person who does so, however, should not hope attain the strength or endurance he or she had in midlife; it is enough just work out for twenty-five minutes three times a week. It would not be realistic suddenly be able to go to downhill ski or tango dance, but one might certainly expect being able to walk a little farther and breathe a little easier with regular conditioning.

As for physical living arrangements, older people are often better off living alone, rather than with their children. Even people with impaired health often can manage live alone. If an older person needs help with housekeeping, he or she should arrange to have this help.

To summarize, senior citizens are often advised taking life easy, but this advice is clearly wrong. Older people should avoid to be alone and should be as social as possible. They can and should have friendships, participate in rewarding activities, and lead active and healthy lives.*

* Based on Richard B. Manchester, *Amazing Facts,* (New York: Bristol Park Books, 1991).

| 7. | **Personalization** |

What do you hope for financially? How and when will you obtain what you hope for? Describe your financial plans for your life. Include some of the phrases in the box, correctly finished with infinitives.

My financial plans for the immediate future are . . .

Five years from now I hope . . .

At that time, I won't expect . . .

However, in ten years hopefully I will be able to afford . . .

To afford this, I will need . . .

I will also be required . . .

In forty years, I will want . . .

When I retire, I intend . . .

UNIT

12

Adverb
Clauses
▼

1. Identifying Adverb Clauses

World Review *interviewed Dr. Milton Scope, a professor of sociology and an expert in what makes happy families. Underline all the adverb clauses in the interview and indicate what kind each is by giving it one of the following labels:* reason, contrast, condition, time, place, comparison, result.

W🌐RLD REVIEW

WR: Dr. Scope, just what *does* make a happy family?

SCOPE: There is a cliche that all happy families have some things in common. <u>While this may be trite</u>, *contrast* it is also true.

WR: Really? What are these things?

SCOPE: Well, in happy families, although family members may argue, they have a basic concern for each other. This factor is very important because every person needs to know that somebody cares for and about him or her.

WR: Is this caring enough to keep young people from turning to criminal acts and violence?

SCOPE: No. Of course it's not that simple, but if a person feels connected to another, he or she is more likely to act in socially acceptable ways.

WR: So, is being connected the principal factor?

SCOPE: It is important.

WR: Tell us what else is important.

SCOPE: When family members have goals and support each other's goals, the family feels united.

WR: Give us an example.

SCOPE: Well, if a parent is hoping to be promoted at work, everybody is supportive and shows interest. If a youngster is trying to make the basketball team, the other family members show encouragement and warmth.

WR: What happens in times of trouble?

SCOPE: When one family member is having trouble, the others should exhibit concern and try to help. Suppose, for example, that someone is fired from a job. Even though this person doesn't have a job, he or she should still feel valued by the rest of the family. In fact, precisely because this person doesn't have a job, he or she *needs* to feel valued.

WR: So, is that the key word, *valued*?

SCOPE: I think it is. People need to feel valued, appreciated. They also need to feel secure among the family members. They need to feel so secure that they know their families will always be there for them.

WR: Does the economic status of the family matter?

SCOPE: Of course, economic stability is favorable. But happy families exist wherever you look, in all economic strata. And unhappy families as well.

2. Using Adverb Clauses

Read the following captions for items included in a mail-order catalog sent out around Christmas time. Complete each caption by filling in the blanks with the item in the box that will form an appropriate adverb clause.

when you want	wherever he goes	so fascinating that
if she likes	less than	as soon as
because it is necessary for her		less expensive than

1. _Because it is necessary for her_ to have a computer for all her work, even when she travels, you must get her this exceptional new laptop.

2. For the whole family, this deluxe picnic cooler will prove perfect _____ the warmer weather arrives.

(continued on next page)

3. _____ on his business trips, he will want to take this

compact suitcase on wheels.

4. For the home, this wide-screen television with stereo is _____

ever before.

5. _____ to tell her that you love her very much and want

to marry her, present her with a beautiful diamond like this.

6. Our new lightweight aluminum fishing rod weighs _____

any other fishing rod and will make him a very happy fisherman.

7. _____ to prepare many kinds of interesting dishes,

delight her with this versatile food processor.

8. For the children, our 1,000-piece set of interlocking plastic pieces will be

_____ your little ones will be kept occupied for hours.

3. Using Adverb Clauses

The following is a recorded message for an airline ticket office. Complete the message by filling in the blanks with the words from the box that correctly introduce the adverb clauses. Use each item only once.

as soon as	if	until
because	so	wherever
even though	than	while

Thank you for calling Global Airlines. _____ _Because_ _____ the demand for our new,
1.

affordable fares is so heavy, our agents are not available to assist you now. Please be patient.

_____ an agent is available, you will be connected. _____
2.   3.

you are connected, we will keep you entertained with music and will provide some information of

interest to you.

_____ you want to go, you can get there on Global Airlines. You don't
4.

have to put up with winter, _____ it's winter all around you. In fact,
5.

_____ the weather is cold and you don't like it, then a Caribbean vacation may
<u>6.</u>

be just the thing for you. Global has more flights to the Caribbean _____ any
<u>7.</u>

other airline. Make your reservations now _____ the supply of low-fare tickets
<u>8.</u>

lasts. Our fares are _____ reasonable you can take your whole family along
<u>9.</u>

with you.

4. Forming Complex Sentences with Adverb Clauses

*Combine each pair of sentences to form a single complex sentence. Use the
indicated subordinating conjunction, so that the combined sentence will
be logical. Do not change any words in the sentences.*

1. There is a lot of violence today.

   No one can escape being touched by it. (because)

   Because there is a lot of violence today, no one can escape being touched by it.

2. We turn on the television.

   We are bombarded with scenes and stories of violence. (whenever)

   _____

3. We go out.

   We know it is possible that we will become victims of violence. (when)

   _____

4. An ever-increasing amount of money is being spent to combat crime.

   Crime rates have not fallen. (in spite of the fact that)

   _____

5. The public can't agree on how to fight crime.

   There is little that can really be done. (as long as)

   _____

6. We need to understand violence better.

   We are searching for its causes. (because)

   _____

7. Children in strong families tend to become socially responsible citizens.

   We need to take steps to strengthen the family. (since)

   _____

86 ▼ UNIT 12

5.

Read the following draft about the history of sports that was prepared for a parks-department bulletin. Find and correct the ten errors in the use of adverb clauses.

they

When wanted to take a break from the serious business of self-preservation, early humans engaged in some type of sports. The playing of games is an important factor distinguishing the higher orders of living things on the evolutionary scale from the lower ones. While animals on the lower end of the scale they display the least amount of playfulness, those at the higher end display the most. If when we watch amoebas through a microscope or earthworms on the ground, they do not appear to play at all; however, dogs, cats, and certainly dolphins and human children play extensively.

Sports are different from other pastimes because wherever conformity to agreed-upon, prescribed rules is required. Whether the sport it is individual or group, these rules must be followed. And when the rules are defined and agreed on, you have a game.

Stone arrowheads discovered by archaeologists indicate that archery was a hunting skill in primordial days, long before became a popular competitive sport in the third century. Games that were precursors of basketball, soccer, and bowling took place wherever was there enough space for a field. Henry VIII coerced court members into playing tennis. Whenever and wherever they are played, sports engage many in healthy competition.

Today, sports are of so interest that many millions of people play and watch them. Although young people are especially interested in sports, sports are an excellent way to keep them out of trouble. Involvement in sports channels young people's energies towards socially acceptable activities and away from crime. Because that you want to have a place for your children to play, you should support your Parks Department. *

* Based on Richard B. Manchester, *Amazing Facts,* (New York: Bristol Park Books, 1991).

6. Personalization

What do you think are some of the main factors that contribute to crime? Write a short essay giving your views. Include some of the phrases in the box.

> A person may turn to crime if . . .
>
> Whenever people are unemployed, . . .
>
> Because guns are readily available, . . .
>
> There is so much violence on television that . . .
>
> Crime among young people may be increasing because . . .
>
> Where laws are strictly enforced, . . .
>
> Crime will continue to increase unless . . .
>
> We will have much less crime when . . .

_____

_____

_____

_____

_____

_____

_____

_____

_____

_____

_____

_____

_____

_____

_____

_____

_____

_____

1. Identifying Viewpoint, Focus, and Negative Adverbials

Read the following letter. Underline the twenty-nine viewpoint, focus, and negative adverbials.

Dear Ricardo,

I'm <u>really</u> glad that you took the job as night clerk in the hotel. I think things will work out for you. Just be serious, work hard, and study hard. By the time your semester ends, you will have saved up almost enough money to get yourself out of debt.

Unfortunately, life is not going so well for me here in my relationship with Lisa. In fact, I hardly have a relationship with her. I think about only her almost every minute, and now I scarcely see her. Not only does she refuse to go out with me, but she doesn't return my phone calls. Never in my whole life have I met anybody like Lisa, and never have I been so miserable. Obviously, she is not interested in me, and I don't know what I did to turn her off. Maybe she simply got bored with me. Maybe she thinks I'm merely a student in transit and not worth an investment of her time. Luckily, as I told you, I have made some friends here, but rarely do they call me these days, because I seem so depressed all the time. Actually, Ricardo, I really am depressed. I know that there are other girls besides Lisa. A few girls who know me even invited me to their homes for dinner, but clearly, I can't go out with them. I guess I'm just a prisoner of love — an unrequited love.

Frankly, I don't care about anything at all these days. Little does Lisa know how miserable I am, and if she finds out, I guess she won't call me. But, if she does call, even just to say hello, I'll be the happiest man in the world. Only when that happens will I be able to live like a normal person again.

Marco

2. Using Focus Adverbs

Rewrite the sentences in this ad for a political candidate by inserting each focus adverb in an appropriate place—that is, right before the words or phrase it focuses on. (Where items include a second sentence, this sentence is intended to clarify the focus.)

Aren't you fed up with the incompetent and corrupt politicians in office? The time has come to throw the rascals out! Ron Rong and all his cronies have almost ruined our state. But Don Deare has come along just in time to save us! Do you know some of the things Ron Rong has done?

1. He said he wanted to do what was best for the state. (only) He didn't want to do anything else.

   He said he wanted to do only what was best for the state.

2. But he used up the state's money. (really)

   _____

3. He put his cronies in the best jobs. (only) Nobody else got these jobs.

   _____

4. He did everything he could for his cronies; he paid for their so-called business trips. (even)

   _____

5. He did the minimal work. (merely) He never did any more work than that minimum.

   _____

6. He appeared in his office, dispensed favors, and went out to play golf. (simply)

   _____

7. He didn't care about the people of this state. (just)

   _____

8. This state will be saved if you elect Don Deare. (only)

   _____

3.   Using Negative Adverbs

The following sentences are from another ad for the same political candidate.
Rewrite the sentences, inserting the negative adverbs at the beginning and
making any other changes in form that are needed.

1. Don Deare loves the people; he acts to help them. (Not only/but)

   Not only does Don Deare love the people, but he acts to help them.

He works almost 365 days a year.

2. He takes a vacation. (Seldom)

   _____

His wonderful and loving family would like to have him spend more time at home.

3. He is able to spend much time with them. (Rarely)

   _____

Although he is not able to spend enough time with his family, he is a loving and considerate husband and father.

4. He neglects his family. (Never)

   _____

He is an honest man.

5. He would accept a bribe. (On no account)

   _____

He makes informed decisions. He looks at each problem carefully.

6. He makes a decision. (Only then)

   _____

7. People realize how many hours he has volunteered at the shelter for the homeless. (Little)

   _____

8. He thinks of himself first. (Never)

   _____

9. He has served the people very well as a civic volunteer; he will do even more for them as a senator. (Not only/but)

   _____

Vote for Don Deare!

4. Using Viewpoint, Focus, and Negative Adverbials

Read the following speech made to a group of parents. Rewrite the sentences so that they include the adverbs indicated. Where two or three blank lines are given, rewrite the sentence in two or three ways.

Welcome, parents.

1. We are pleased that attention is being focused on the importance of strong families. (certainly)

   A. *Certainly, we are pleased that attention is being focused on the importance of strong families.*

   B. *We are certainly pleased that attention is being focused on the importance of strong families.*

   C. *We are pleased, certainly, that attention is being focused on the importance of strong families.*

2. We agree that steps must be taken to strengthen the family. (clearly)

   _____

3. There is another factor that must be considered, however— the influence of TV violence. (sadly)

   A. _____

   B. _____

4. We encounter scenes of violence wherever we look, in cartoon shows and programs for families. (even)

   _____

5. Our children can't help seeing these scenes. (unfortunately)

   A. _____

   B. _____

   C. _____

6. We must take action to strengthen the family, we must pressure our legislators to stop TV violence.

   (not only/but)

   _____

7. Much needs to be done. (obviously)

   A. _____

   B. _____

   C. _____

8. We will win the war against violent programs. (hopefully)

   A. _____

   B. _____

   C. _____

9. We can limit our children's TV viewing. (fortunately)

   A. _____

   B. _____

   C. _____

(continued on next page)

10. This means allowing programs that do not show violence. (only)

_____

11. Other programs are "off limits." (simply)

_____

12. We also have to help our children develop other interests so they will not be tempted to sit glued to the TV. (at all)

_____

5. Editing

Read the following draft of an article. Find and correct the nineteen errors in the use of viewpoint, focus, and negative adverbials.

This week in Los Angeles, California, the top Scrabble players of the world are locked together in mortal conflict. Scrabble players? Scrabble players, indeed. Here ~~are they~~ *they are*, and they are battling hard really to determine the world's champion. This is a tournament for the only best players of this word game; seldom amateurs appear here. The game of Scrabble is played throughout the world and in six different languages. The object is simply to score as many points as possible by forming words from the individual letters imprinted on little wooden squares. A player hopefully gets many points by making clever combinations of letters according to the rules of the game. The competition at the tournament is as just fierce as that at the World Cup or the Olympic Games. A player never gives nothing to the opposing player; each point is won through only a hard fight.

In playing Scrabble, not only it is necessary to have an extensive vocabulary, but it is also imperative to possess a good imagination and excellent mathematical skills. Mathematical skills? Yes. To obviously know the words is important, but it is more even important to know how just to place the letters on the board and to estimate the probabilities of drawing the letters you want at any given time.

Of the top ten Scrabble players, one only is engaged in a career that requires language skills. Almost all the others are mathematics and computer professionals, and even there is a croupier among them. At all this is not the image we have of people obsessed with words; people obsessed with words are supposed to be writers, poets, and English teachers, not practical and precise mathematical types.

This doesn't mean that mathematical wizards play only this game. At the National Scrabble Tournament, held semiannually in different cities of the United States, one also finds doctors, lawyers, schoolteachers, surfers, truck drivers, business people, retirees, and teenagers, among many others.

One hundred sixty-seven actually different occupations were listed for the 400 people who participated in the last tournament.

Little it is known that this subculture of Scrabble players exists. It surely does exist, though, with its hundreds of participants training and practicing, memorizing lists, and learning strategies as just vigorously as marathon runners preparing for their race.

6. Personalization

How do you think you and one other person could survive for a year in the wilderness? What would you take with you? What would you do? Write a paragraph about this topic. Include some of the phrases in the box.

We will take only . . .	Rarely . . .
We won't even take . . .	Certainly, with strength and a little luck . . .
Fortunately, we are . . .	
During this time, we will just . . .	Hopefully, . . .

_____

_____

_____

_____

_____

_____

_____

_____

_____

_____

_____

_____

_____

_____

_____

UNIT

14

Other Discourse Connectors

▼

1. Identifying Discourse Connectors

Read the following installment of "Around the Stars," a one-minute television spot about news and gossip from Hollywood. Underline the twenty-one discourse connectors.

Good evening, ladies and gentlemen. We are here to bring you the latest news from Hollywood.

First, a major new studio has been created. The three biggest motion picture producers have just joined forces to form a new studio. As a result, Bigthree Productions, as it is going to be named, will be the largest studio ever in Hollywood. Moreover, it has more money behind it than any studio in Hollywood has ever had. In addition, seven megastars have joined the group as limited partners; therefore, they will have a financial interest in the success of the company. Bigthree Productions is expected to produce excellent financial results even at the beginning. However, there are several lawsuits pending against the three partners from the complicated business dealings they had with their previous studios. In fact, one of the lawsuits has been brought by the first ex-wife of one of the partners, who claims that her husband owes her $7 million for her starring role in *Imelda*.

Next, we have reports that movie queen Rosalinda Rock has finally found happiness. Yes, she and actor Fox Craft were married secretly last month in a small town in Nevada. There had been reports that Fox was involved with an Italian starlet, but these reports have turned out to be false. Rosalinda and Fox are getting a beachfront house in Santa Monica and a ranch near Sun Valley, so they will have a choice about where to spend their time between movies. Fox gave Rosalinda a diamond-and-emerald necklace as a wedding present; besides that, he had apparently given her a ten-carat diamond ring several weeks earlier. Rosalinda says she wants to have many children and stay home, at one of her homes, to take care of them; nevertheless, she is off to Tahiti next week for several months on location.

Finally, nobody can predict this year who the winners of the Academy Awards are going to be. For one thing, the pictures this year were better than ever before. The adventure story *Running in Space* has stunned everyone with its special effects, and it has impressed the critics with its incredible plot. It's a definite contender for the best picture award, along with *Love at the Turn of the Century,* which moved even the most macho of men to tears. On the other hand, the award could go to any one of several fine comedies, or the brilliant horror movie *Drackenstein* might be the first of its genre to win.

The suspense over the Academy Awards is tremendous, and everybody is eagerly awaiting the big night. Meanwhile, join us again every night at 9:00 to learn more of what's really going on Around the Stars.

2. Using Discourse Connectors

Read the following letter, written by a freshman in college. Complete the letter by filling in the blanks with discourse connectors from the box. (Each connector should be used once.) Do not change punctuation.

however	but	as a result	in contrast
third	first	to sum up	and
for example	also	second	

Dear Mom and Dad,

It's great to be here on campus. _____However_____, there is something I really need, and
1.
that is a car.

The town does have a bus, _____ this bus comes very infrequently.
2.
_____, I've found myself in three undesirable situations. _____, I've been
3.   4.
stuck in the dorm. _____, I've gotten rides with other people and have had to go when
5.
and where they wanted to go. _____, I've walked into town and taken hours to do
6.
what I could have done in minutes. On Saturday, _____, I spent all day buying some
7.
groceries. _____, not having a car has been extremely inconvenient.
8.
With a car, _____, life would be easy, _____ I would probably have
9.   10.
much more time to do my schoolwork. _____, with a car I could come visit you more often.
11.
Please give this matter some thought, Mom and Dad. I'll call you on Sunday.

Your loving daughter,

Nicole

3. Using Discourse Connectors

Complete the following article by filling in each blank with the correct discourse connector.

HURRICANES AND EARTHQUAKES

Hurricanes and earthquakes are similar in that they both cause extensive damage.

_____*However*_____, an earthquake is even more terrifying than a hurricane just because it
1. (However / Because of / In addition)

strikes so suddenly. An earthquake gives no warning, _____ there is plenty of warning
2. (and / but / or)

before a hurricane. Weather satellites, _____, send signals enabling the
3. (in fact / in conclusion / on the other hand)

weather bureau to issue warnings several days in advance of a hurricane. _____,
4. (As a result / On the contrary / Yet)

people can prepare for hurricanes by stocking up on food and supplies and securing their property.

_____, there is enough time for people who live near the coastal areas to
5. (Furthermore / However / Consequently)

evacuate to higher land if they are advised to do so by the authorities._____,
6. (Consequently / Therefore / In contrast)

because earthquakes give no warning, preparation is impossible. _____, many
7. (Moreover / Therefore / After that)

buildings in earthquake zones are not built strongly enough to withstand the shock waves of a strong

quake, _____ they are vulnerable to damage. People are not safe in their homes,
8. (instead / so / but)

_____ can they seek safety on the highways, which can also be damaged by the shock waves.
9. (or / nor / and)

4. Using Discourse Connectors

Complete the following by filling in each blank with the correct discourse connector. Take the punctuation into consideration.

Dear Marco,

Now I'm really worried about you. I'm the one who's always asking for advice,

_____*and*_____ you're the one who's always giving it. _____,
1. (and / additionally)   2. (Also / Instead)

this time I find myself advising you.

_____, no matter what, you have to get a hold of yourself.
3. (First / Next)

_____, you are going to spiral downward and feel worse and worse.
4. (Therefore / Otherwise)

_____, you won't be effective in this downbeat mood that you're in.
5. (However / In addition)

_____ 6. (And / But) _____ 7. (first / finally), Lisa or any other young woman you

may meet is going to find you a drag, _____ 8. (however / so) you'll definitely find

yourself without a girlfriend.

_____ 9. (Despite / On the contrary) feeling so bad, you've got to get out in the world again.

_____ 10. (However / For instance), you should take one of the young women up on her offer to

invite you to dinner. Who knows? _____ 11. (Along with / Likewise) having a good dinner, you

might find a really pleasant relationship.

    Now, enough about you. Let's get back to me. I got fired. I was doing everything

right, _____ 12. (finally / but) I still got fired. It was a terrible experience.

_____ 13. (Thus / Besides), it couldn't have happened at a worse time: I'd just found out my

landlord is raising the rent.

    Hope to hear some better news from you.

                Ricardo

5. Editing

Read the following draft of a composition for a freshman English class. Find and correct the eleven errors in the use of discourse connectors. Replace the incorrect discourse connectors; do not change word order or punctuation.

    I like to play football for a lot of reasons.

    First, I like the teamwork. It really feels good to be part of a group whose

members depend on each other. For example, when I throw the ball to a receiver on

my team, I know that there's a good chance he's going to catch it. It takes both of

us to make the catch work. ~~Accordingly~~ _Because of_ my good throwing ability, the ball is usually

on target; however, the receiver also has to be in position and has to make

(continued on next page)

the catch. Because, our score is due in part to me as the quarterback, in part to the receiver, and in part to the other members of the team.

Second, I like the competition. I like the feeling of playing to win; and, I like the sense of fighting the other team.

Third, I like the physical exercise. I think pushing myself to my physical limit is good for my body. I am not afraid of overdoing the exercise, or do I have fears of being hurt during a game, however the fact that many quarterbacks get hurt.

Finally, I like the glory. I love it when the crowd roars to encourage us, also I love it when I hear the cheerleaders shouting my name. It sure makes a guy feel important to be recognized around town as a big hero.

Are there any drawbacks? Yes. It's terrific to play football, nevertheless there are some negative aspects. Being part of a team is great; but, you don't have much of a private life. Playing in competition is exciting. Although, you don't get much chance to relax. In fact, there's a negative aspect to each of the things I like about football, but these drawbacks are relatively unimportant.

In conclusion, I like being a football player consequently the teamwork, the competition, the physical exercise, and the glory.

6. Personalization

Participation in sports is often required in schools and colleges. Some people think that these activities should not be compulsory. Write a three-paragraph essay about the pros and cons of requiring participation in sports. Include the sentences given below, and use some of the discourse connectors in the box.

Discourse connectors:

	Moreover	Despite	Otherwise	Second
In addition	For example/instance	In contrast	As a result	Finally
Furthermore	However	Therefore	First	

Paragraph 1: There are certain reasons why schools should require participation in sports activities.

Paragraph 2: On the other hand, there are also reasons why participation in sports activities should not be required.

Paragraph 3: I think the advantages of requiring participation outweigh the disadvantages. OR I think the disadvantages of requiring participation outweigh the advantages.

Paragraph 3
last sentence: In conclusion, . . .

_____

_____

_____

_____

_____

_____

_____

_____

_____

_____

_____

_____

_____

_____

_____

_____

_____

_____

_____

_____

1. Identifying Adverbial Modifying Phrases

Read the following editorial article from a local newspaper and underline the adverbial modifying phrases.

O ur beautiful city, Beautiville, has become too popular. Known for its clean air, friendly people, excellent transportation, and safe streets, Beautiville naturally tends to attract newcomers. We in Beautiville are proud of our city's reputation but—and this is a big but—are concerned that its population has doubled in only five years. While struggling with the demands presented by a population grown too fast, the government has attempted to serve everybody well. However, these attempts have been inadequate, creating more problems than solutions. Having caused such strains that our government can no longer effectively serve us, this increase in population now should be limited.

How can we do this? We can do it by limiting the number of high-density buildings permitted to be built in certain areas. We can do it by discouraging outsiders from investing in our city. By taking concrete measures like these, we can effectively limit our growth. Faced with a tough choice between limiting our population and letting our standards of living slip, we must take positive steps and preserve the excellent quality of life that we have here in Beautiville.

2. Using Adverbial Modifying Phrases

Read the following passage (a continuation of the "Hurricanes and Earthquakes" article in Unit 14). Complete the article by filling in each blank with the correct words.

Both hurricanes and earthquakes can severely disrupt normal

life _____*by damaging*_____ the infrastructure in the area.
    1. (by damaging / having damaging / damage)

_____ cut off, the electricity, the telephones, and the
2. (Been / Having been / To be)

water service remain nonfunctioning, sometimes for several weeks after the event has occurred.

_____ its electricity, the community has no refrigeration, and so keeping
3. (By lost / Having been lost / Having lost)

food safe from contamination becomes a serious problem. _____ a
4. (To ensure / By ensuring / Having ensured)

continuous supply of vital electricity, hospitals are equipped with generators that can provide

it in the event of a power outage. Without electricity, the traffic signals might not function, and

_____ these signals, drivers frequently have accidents and create traffic
5. (not having / not having had / not to have)

jams. When _____ so continuously, people often act rudely to each other,
6. (stressed / stressing / having stressed)

further _____ the discomfort.
7. (spreading / spread / having spread)

To summarize, the widespread loss of electricity and other services following a disaster such

as a hurricane or an earthquake affects people very seriously, often _____
8. (having brought / bringing / to bring)

chaos to the community.

3. Forming Sentences with Adverbial Phrases

Combine each pair of sentences to make a single sentence, in which the first sentence becomes an adverbial phrase and the second sentence an independent clause. Use present participles, past participles, and **having** *plus past participles as appropriate. You may move the noun subject to the second clause to replace the subject. Do not add any words.*

1. Many people try to stay healthy. They quickly adopt the latest health recommendations.

   Trying to stay healthy, many people quickly adopt the latest health recommendations.

2. People were told that vitamin C, vitamin E, and beta-carotene greatly reduce cancer risk. They began buying these nutrients in large quantities.

   _____

   _____

3. People were informed that taking one aspirin a day lessens the chances of having a heart attack. They began taking aspirin.

   _____

   _____

(continued on next page)

4. Many people learned that one glass of wine per day has a beneficial effect on the heart and circulatory system. They now drink wine for medicinal reasons.

_____

_____

5. People hope to lower their cholesterol levels. They minimize their intake of animal fats.

_____

_____

6. People know that roughage in the diet is excellent for digestion. They are consuming more fresh fruit, vegetables, and whole wheat products.

_____

_____

7. Some people believe that eating a lot of fish will raise their intelligence level. They eat a lot of fish.

_____

_____

8. People have known for a long time that too much salt and sugar is unhealthful. They buy a lot of salt-free and sugar-free products.

_____

_____

9. People realize that they can contribute to their own good health. They eat much more knowledgeably than they used to.

_____

_____

4. Editing

The following message greets new users of a computer communications program.
Find and correct the eleven errors in the adverbial phrases.

Welcome to the wonderful world of Globe Probe! With our computer communications program you will quickly be able to find exactly what you want just by click*ing* on the easily identifiable icon for your area of interest. Found more information, games, and new friends than you ever dreamed of, you will enter a brand new life. Hit *Enter* to continued with this message.

After having complete the tour of what's available on Globe Probe, explore each of our departments. What are your interests? Sports? When look around to find the latest on sports, you will find discussion groups, news groups, and hot-off-the-press scores in our sports department. Finance? Get the business news as well as the latest in stock quotes.

Scroll through a listing of 103 of America's most popular publications. Having find the publication you want, peruse the article titles and just click on your choice. Shopping? Movie reviews? Concerts? Book reviews? Travel? Just to clicking on *Imprints*, you will immediately be able to read reviews of the newest happenings by the most knowledgeable writers in their fields.

Then, participate in one or more of our clubs: the environment, astronomy, foreign affairs, science fiction, and twenty-eight more. You will find hundreds of other people with the same interests. Having join a club, you will encounter a whole new world of friends and communication.

Our encyclopedia is the most comprehensive of all the online services. When require to find facts fast, simply access the topic you want to know about—the latest research on tooth decay, for example, or what the capital of Belize is—and you'll find the facts you need.

Have obtained the facts so quickly and easily, you will be amazed by how much you can learn while have a lot of fun at the same time. Globe Probe immeasurably enriches your life from the first moment that you use it.

Hit the space bar to view the Globe Probe menu.

5. Personalization

What are your career goals for the next ten years? Write a short essay about what your goals are and how you will achieve them. Include some of the adverbial clauses in the box. Be sure to avoid dangling modifiers.

When thinking about my career goals for the next ten years, . . .

Having thought about my career goals for the next ten years, . . .

If given the opportunity . . .

By working hard, . . .

When given a job to do, . . .

If forced to do boring or unpleasant tasks, . . .

While performing my duties, . . .

To gain recognition, . . .

Having achieved my goals, . . .

Hoping to improve even further, . . .

1. Identifying Adjective Clauses

Read the following article about an invention and its inventor. Underline all the adjective clauses. (Remember, some adjective clauses do not have a relative pronoun.)

What do you know about Liquid Paper? Liquid Paper is the white liquid <u>that covers up the mistakes</u> you make when writing or typing. It was invented by Bette Nesmith Graham, a secretary in Dallas in the early 1950s, who began using tempera paint to cover up her typing errors.

At the time, she was a 27-year-old single mother of one son, struggling to make ends meet and working as a secretary to the chairman of a big Dallas bank. When she found herself confronted with her first electric typewriter, whose ink didn't erase as cleanly as that of manual typewriters, Ms. Nesmith, who was also an artist, quietly began painting out her mistakes. Soon she was supplying bottles of her homemade preparation, which she called Mistake Out, to other secretaries in the building.

When she lost her job with the company, she turned to working full-time to develop the Mistake Out as a business, expanding from her house into a small trailer she had bought for the backyard. In hopes of marketing her product, she approached IBM, which turned her down. She stepped up her own marketing and within a decade was a financial success. The product, which came to be called Liquid Paper, was manufactured in four countries and sold in nearly three dozen. In fiscal 1979, which ended about six months before she sold the company, it had sales of $38 million, of which $3.5 million was net income. By the time she finally sold her business to Gillette in 1979, she had built her simple, practical idea into a $47.5 million business.

It is heartwarming that the story has a happy ending in more ways than one. Ms. Nesmith remarried and became Mrs. Graham. Her son, Michael, a musician of whom she is understandably proud, became very successful as one of a music group called "The Monkees," which appeared on an NBC television show for several years in the mid-1960s.

(continued on next page)

Subsequently a country-rock musician, a songwriter, and a video producer, he now heads a production company in California, where he also directs some charities.

With some of her profits, Mrs. Graham established a foundation whose purpose is to provide leading intellectuals with the time, space, and compatible colleagues that they need to ponder and articulate the most important social problems of our era. Bette Nesmith Graham first developed a product that there was clearly a need for; then she used the substantial profits for charitable purposes, which is a fine thing to do.*

*Based on an article by Eric Morgenthaler from, *The Wall Street Journal,* July 29, 1994.

2. Using Relative Pronouns

*Complete the article by filling in the blanks with appropriate relative pronouns from the box. Where more than one selection is possible, write all the possibilities, including **0** if no relative pronoun is needed.*

who	which	that
whom	whose	when
where	0	

Dr. Jennifer Wise has obtained a grant of $17 million for her research on the factors affecting the natural resistance *that / which / 0* the human body has
1.
to cold viruses. Dr. Wise has investigated the common beliefs about catching colds to _____ people have long
2.
subscribed—for example, the beliefs that colds come from sitting in places _____ there is a draft, going
3.
out with wet hair, not wearing warm enough clothing, and sitting near a person _____ is coughing and
4.
sneezing.

She discredits all these ideas as having no merit but says that there are other factors _____ 5. actually contribute to catching a cold. For example, her research has shown that you can catch a cold from a person _____ 6. you have been near just from touching him or her or something _____ 7. he or she has touched, so it is important and effective to wash your hands frequently and well.

Second, not getting the rest _____ 8. your body needs lowers resistance. People _____ 9. sleep patterns don't provide them with enough deep sleep will more easily catch a cold than people _____ 10. get enough rest. Deep sleep is especially important at times _____ 11. people are under more stress than usual.

Third, she has found some evidence that taking high doses of vitamin C, _____ 12. has been controversial for some time, actually does seem to raise resistance.

As for treating the common cold: Nothing will cure it, but there are some palliative steps _____ 13. may be taken. You may take aspirin and other medications _____ 14. act to relieve your discomfort, stay in bed if you can, drink plenty of liquids, and partake of the home remedy _____ 15. has been around for centuries: the chicken soup _____ 16. your mother makes.

3. Using Adjective Clauses

Write sentences describing ten objects that are part of modern life. First match each item in column I with the appropriate item in column II. Then, for each pair of matched items, write a sentence that uses an adjective clause to describe the object. (Some adjective clauses may be written in more than one way.)

I	II
1. A cellular phone/wireless telephone	A. transmits written material instantly by telephone
2. A beeper/battery-operated device	B. it records telephone messages
3. An air bag/device in a car	C. it records TV shows for viewing at a future time
4. A microwave oven/oven	D. you find words in it by punching in their letters
5. A fax machine/machine	E. it inflates upon collision to prevent injury
6. A computer/electronic device	F. people use it to speak to others from their cars
7. A CD/small disc	G. its function is to store and process data
8. An answering machine/electronic device	H. its beeping noise indicates when someone is trying to make a phone connection with you
9. An electronic dictionary/gadget	I. music is recorded on it
10. A VCR/machine	J. people cook food quickly in it

1. _F. A cellular telephone is a wireless telephone that people use to speak to others from their cars._

2. _____

3. _____

4. _____

5. _____

6. _____

7. _____

_____

8. _____

_____

9. _____

_____

10. _____

_____

4. Distinguishing between Identifying and Nonidentifying Clauses

Read the following sentences about the Moonrise Film Festival. Each of the sentences contains an adjective clause of either the identifying or nonidentifying type. For each, decide whether (A) or (B) describes the first sentence. Pay special attention to punctuation.

1. Moviegoers, who appreciate fine films, were very satisfied with the Moonrise Film Festival this year.

   (A.) Moviegoers in general appreciate fine films.

   B. Only some moviegoers appreciate fine films.

2. Moviegoers who appreciate fine films were very satisfied with the Moonrise Film Festival this year.

   A. Moviegoers in general appreciate fine films.

   B. Only some moviegoers appreciate fine films.

3. The films, which were chosen for their artistry in cinematography, left vivid and lasting impressions.

   A. The films in general left vivid and lasting impressions.

   B. Only some films left vivid and lasting impressions.

4. The films that were chosen for their artistry in cinematography left vivid and lasting impressions.

   A. The films in general left vivid and lasting impressions.

   B. Only some films left vivid and lasting impressions.

5. Offbeat films brought critical acclaim to directors, who are normally very profit oriented.

   A. Directors in general are normally very profit oriented.

   B. Only some directors are normally very profit oriented.

(continued on next page)

6. Offbeat films brought critical acclaim to directors who are normally very profit oriented.

   A. Directors in general are normally very profit oriented.

   B. Only some directors are normally very profit oriented.

7. In the animation category, the audience was surprised and satisfied by Hollywood's new-style cartoons, which address serious social concerns.

   A. Hollywood's new-style cartoons in general address social concerns.

   B. Only some of Hollywood's new-style cartoons address social concerns.

8. In the animation category, the audience was surprised and satisfied by Hollywood's new-style cartoons that address serious social concerns.

   A. Hollywood's new-style cartoons in general address social concerns.

   B. Only some of Hollywood's new-style cartoons address social concerns.

9. The foreign entries, which were brilliantly directed, unfortunately may not succeed at the box office here.

   A. The foreign entries in general were brilliantly directed.

   B. Only some of the foreign entries were brilliantly directed.

10. Only the documentaries, which proved to be disappointing this year, represented a poor selection.

    A. The documentaries in general were a poor selection.

    B. Only some of the documentaries were a poor selection.

11. We hope to see further works from the new entrants from the African countries whose film industries are just emerging.

    A. The film industries in African countries in general are just emerging.

    B. The film industries in some African countries are just emerging.

12. If such excellence in selection and presentation continues, the Moonrise Film Festival will soon take its place among the film festivals of the world that rival Cannes.

    A. Film festivals in general rival Cannes.

    B. Only some film festivals rival Cannes.

5. Editing

In the following article, find and correct the eighteen errors in the formation of the adjective clauses.

One of the ways in ~~whom~~ *in which* people can be classified is by labeling them extroverts and introverts. However, there are other methods, some of them are now considered to have little scientific value, that people use to conveniently pigeonhole members of the human race.

For example, there is the division into mesomorphs, who are muscular; endomorphs, who tend to be fat; and ectomorphs, who are thin. The endomorph is stereotyped as a relaxed and unobsessive personality, whereas the ectomorph is stereotyped as a person whom is nervous and serious and whom rarely smiles.

A further facile division is made by defining people as Type A and Type B. Type A describes people to which everything is serious and who they are very ambitious and driving. Type A originally described people, usually middle-aged males, whom often suffered heart attacks. Type B, on the other hand, labels a rather passive, ambitionless person of that others frequently take advantage, and which is probably not a candidate for a heart attack.

Some people categorize human beings by the astrological sign that they were born under it. For example, a person who born between April 22 and May 21 is called a Taurus and is supposed to possess certain characteristics such as congeniality and tact. A person that born between June 22 and July 21 is a Cancer and is reputed to be stubborn but effective. There are twelve such categories, which encompass all the months of the year. Many people base their lives and relationships on the predictions made by astrologers.

One recent theory to categorize people is the theory of left-brained and right-brained people. Right-brained people, that are intuitive and romantic, are the artists and creative people of the world according to this theory. Left-brained people, who they are logical in their thinking, turn out to be mathematicians and scientists. According to this theory, people whose their functioning is not developed enough in the areas they would like can act to develop the side of the brain they want to improve it in order to better balance their personality.

All of these theories, which in themselves are too simplistic, are indeed unscientific. However, they have provided attractive and sometimes amusing solutions for people are looking for easy ways to understand the human race. Different theories of categorizing people, which it is always a difficult thing to do, will continue to come and go.

6. Personalization

Write a description of the kind of person you would like to marry. If you are married, pretend you are not and describe an imaginary ideal person. Include some of the phrases in the box, appropriately finished with adjective clauses.

> I'd like to marry a person who . . .
>
> This will be a person whom . . .
>
> My ideal person will be someone whose . . .
>
> We will have a marriage that . . .
>
> We will have a home we . . .
>
> I look forward to a wonderful life with my husband/wife, who . . .

_____

_____

_____

_____

_____

_____

_____

_____

_____

_____

_____

_____

_____

_____

_____

_____

_____

Adjective
Clauses with
Quantifiers;
Adjectival
Modifying
Phrases

▼

1. Identifying Adjective Clauses and Adjective Phrases

In the following passage, underline the adjective clauses and circle the adjective phrases.

The movie industry, (barely born before the turn of the century,) began

producing silent films in the early 1900s. Filmmakers, learning how to fake

prizefights, news events, and foreign settings, increased the length and variety

of their films. Some of the early filmmakers, however, actually provided

coverage of certain news events, <u>among which were the inauguration of</u>

<u>President William McKinley and the action at the front in the Boer War</u>.

Travelogues, many of which were filmed in remote parts of the world, became

very popular, as did short science films, made with the aid of the microscope.

One of the important technical film pioneers was French magician

Georges Méliès, credited with creating methods leading toward the

development of special-effects movies. He used innovative techniques,

examples of which include double exposure, mattes, slow and fast motion,

animation, and miniature models. Through these techniques, he was able to

create popular film fantasies, one of which was called *A Trip to the Moon* and

influenced many subsequent filmmakers.

At the same time, filmmakers in England were developing fiction films

shot outdoors, some of which involved chase scenes. In 1903, Edwin S. Porter, a

camera operator and director, made *The Great Train Robbery,* a movie showing

different actions simultaneously. For some chase scenes, Porter mounted a

camera in a car of a train. Along with bringing excitement and suspense to the

movies, Porter firmly established the genre of the chase film, seen and loved

even today.

Thus began the era of the silent film, changing the world forever.

2. Forming Adjective Clauses with Quantifiers

The following sentences present some interesting facts. Complete these sentences
by writing adjective clauses with quantifiers (or other expressions of quantity)
+ preposition + relative pronoun.*

1. The average American's diet contains quite a bit of sodium, *most of which comes from processed food*.
   (most / come / from processed food)

2. In the past 20 years in Florida, insects, spiders, and alligators have caused 82 deaths,

   _____.
   (most / could / have / be avoided)

3. Hospital stays in Japan, _____, are far longer than hospital stays
   (half / be / longer than / 40 days)
   in the United States.

4. According to survey results, Americans today, _____,
   (71 percent / think / people in power take advantage of others)
   feel more victimized than did Americans in the past.

5. According to intelligence test results, stutterers, _____,
   (14 percent / achieve scores of over 130 on IQ tests)
   appear to be smarter than nonstutterers.

6. The hearing impaired, _____, are a more diverse group than is
   (more than half / be / under 64 years old)
   sometimes thought.

7. Vegetables, _____, can be microwaved, stir-fried,
   (all / yield / more nutrients when lightly cooked than when raw)
   or quick-steamed.

8. Americans eat an average of 21.5 pounds per year of food between meals,

   _____.
   (much / be / junk food)

* The information is taken from *Health,* October 1993 and November–December 1994.

3. Reducing Adjective Clauses to Adjective Phrases

*Read the following descriptions of movies from a publication for TV viewers.
Change the adjective clauses in parentheses to adjective phrases.*

1. ROCKY II

In the sequel to the 1976 blockbuster, heavyweight Rocky Balboa gets a rematch in this action

thriller, *written and directed by and again starring Sylvester Stallone*_____
   (which was written and directed by and again stars Sylvester Stallone)

_____.

2. INDOCHINE

This is an Oscar-winning chronicle of French colonialism, _____

_____.
   (which is embodied by Catherine Deneuve as a plantation owner)

3. JEZEBEL

Bette Davis won an Oscar for her portrayal of a pre–Civil War southern vixen who causes

problems for the unfortunate people _____
(who surround her)

_____.

4. BEAUTY AND THE BEAST

This superlative animated musical from Disney tells of the romance between a beautiful young

girl and a prince _____
(who has been transformed by a magic spell)

_____.

5. THE BIG CHILL

Fine ensemble acting distinguishes Lawrence Kasdan's story of college friends _____

_____.
(who have been reunited for a funeral)

6. BORN FREE

This is a touching, fact-based heartwarmer about a couple _____
(who is raising a lion cub in Kenya)

_____.

7. DAVE

Kevin Kline plays a dual role in this political satire about an employment agency owner

_____
(who has been enlisted to impersonate the president of the United States)

_____.

8. FAR AND AWAY

Tom Cruise and Nicole Kidman play an Irish tenant farmer and a landowner's feisty daughter,

_____
(who fall into trouble as they immigrate to America)

_____.

9. FREE WILLY

An orphan befriends a neglected killer whale _____
(which is held in captivity)

_____.

10. GORILLAS IN THE MIST

Sigourney Weaver portrays naturalist Dian Fossey, _____
(who fought to save Africa's gorillas from extinction)

_____.

11. HOME ALONE 2

This sequel finds Kevin, _____
(who is again separated from his vacationing family)

and _____, in various adventures.
(who faces similar woes)

12. HOWARDS END

This is an adaptation of E.M. Forster's Edwardian novel about two British sisters _____

_____.
(who become involved with a wealthy family)

4. Adjective Clauses with Quantifiers and Using Adjective Phrases

Read the following pairs of sentences. For each pair of sentences, combine the second sentence with the first one. Use an adjective phrase or, if the second sentence has a quantifier, an adjective clause with a quantifier.

If you are going to buy a computer, you must be aware of several things.

1. First, there are two basic types of personal computers. These two types of personal computers are the IBM (or IBM-compatible) and the Macintosh.

   First, there are two basic types of personal computers, the IBM (or IBM-compatible) and the Macintosh.

2. Then, there are various places where you can buy computers. These places include computer stores, electronics stores, office-supply stores, and mail-order houses.

   _____

   _____

3. At reasonable prices you can get everything you need. The prices range from $1,200 to $3,000.

   _____

   _____

4. Within this price range, of course, you will find varying capabilities among the computers. Many of the computers come equipped with a fax/modem.

   _____

   _____

5. Many major brands of computer have a toll-free number. This number is given to customers so that they may call the company for technical assistance.

   _____

   _____

6. If you are a new buyer, you should buy from a store where you know you can get help. A new buyer has little experience with computers.

   _____

   _____

7. While you are shopping around, you will find words like *hard drive, megabyte,* and *CD-ROM drive.* These words are all part of a computer owner's vocabulary.

   _____

   _____

8. If you need your computer while you are traveling, you should consider a laptop. A laptop is small enough and light enough to carry with you.

_____

_____

9. Sometimes computers come with programs. The programs have already been installed at the factory.

_____

_____

10. You don't have to buy many extra capabilities right away. The capabilities are unneeded by beginners.

_____

_____

11. For newcomers to computers, it's a good idea to take some classes or to get a tutor. Both of these can usually be arranged by the store.

_____

_____

5. Editing

Read the following passage on films after World War II. Find and correct the fifteen errors involving adjective clauses and phrases. Delete, fix, or replace words, but do not change punctuation or add words.

After World War II, Europe was the center of important developments in filmmaking, which ~~they~~ strongly influenced motion pictures worldwide. In Italy, well-known movies, some of them were Rossellini's *Open City,* making in 1945, and De Sica's *Shoeshine* (1946) and *Bicycle Thief* (1948), established a trend toward realism in film. These directors weren't concerned with contrived plots or stories that produced for entertainment value alone; they took their cameras into the streets to make films showed the harshness of life in the years after the war. In the next decades, Federico Fellini, was an outstanding director, combined realistic plots with poetic imagery, symbolism, and philosophical ideas in now-classic films, the most famous of them is *La Strada,* which a movie ostensibly about circus people in the streets but really about the meaning of life.

In France, a group of young filmmakers, calling the "New Wave," appeared during the 1950s.

(continued on next page)

This group developed a new kind of focus, which stressed characterization rather than plot, and new camera and acting techniques, seeing in movies such as Truffaut's *400 Blows*. In England, another group of filmmakers, was known as the "Angry Young Man" movement, developed a new realism. In Sweden, Ingmar Bergman used simple stories and allegories to look at complex philosophical and social issues, some of them are masterfully explored in *The Seventh Seal*. The Spaniard Luis Buñuel depicted social injustices and used surrealistic techniques, creating films like *Viridiana*.

Postwar developments in filmmaking were not limited to Western Europe. The Japanese director Akira Kurosawa, was the first Asian filmmaker to have a significant influence in Europe, made *Rashomon* in 1950. Movies from India, like Satyajit Ray's *Pather Panchali*, showed us life on the subcontinent. Even in Russia, where filmmaking was under state control, it was possible to make movies like *The Cranes Are Flying*, portray the problems of the individual. Russian directors also made films based on literary classics, included Shakespeare's plays and Tolstoi's monumental historical novel, *War and Peace*.

In summary, in the decades after World War II, filmmaking turned in new directions, as shown by a wide range of movies from around the world, many of them focused on the meaning of life and how to interpret it.

6. Personalization

What was the best movie that you have ever seen? What can you remember about it? Write a short essay about the movie. Begin with this sentence: **One of my favorite movies is _____.** *Include some of the phrases in the boxes.*

> I liked the movie for a number of reasons, some of which are . . .
>
> The movie had some good actors, including . . .
>
> The movie had some really exciting (funny) scenes, examples of which are . . .
>
> I remember the scene taking place . . .
>
> There was an exciting plot, involving . . .
>
> The movie had an interesting ending, resulting in . . .

The director was _____, also known for directing . . .

I like his (her) movies, all of which . . .

The movie won some awards, including . . .

I would have no trouble recommending this movie, one of the . . .

Perhaps this movie will be shown again soon, in which case . . .

1. Identifying Noun Clauses

Read the following from an organization that promotes peace. Underline the noun clauses.

"There is many a boy here today who looks on war as glory, but boys, it is all hell." Are these words the words of a pacifist, of a conscientious objector, who believes <u>that wars should not be fought by people who don't believe in war</u>? No, this is an utterance by General William Tecumseh Sherman, a Union general in the American Civil War, who is remembered for his devastating march through the American South, and who had often stated unequivocally that ruthlessness in modern war is necessary.

Who fights in wars? Who thinks that sacrificing one's life and the lives of others is glorious? While many enter the service as a career, or with patriotic zeal during a war, many more are conscripted by their governments. This means compulsory enrollment in the armed forces, in war or in peace. That all a nation's able-bodied men give compulsory military service was an idea introduced in the late eighteenth century during the French Revolution; it enabled Napoleon, several years later, to raise huge armies. This kind of system, in which the government conscripted whoever was able, was adopted by other European countries during the nineteenth century. What took place in the United States was wartime conscription during the Civil War and in both world wars, as well as a draft maintained from 1945 to 1973.

Our organization asks why people go to war. We question whether any territorial imperative, commercial advantage, or religious belief can justify the loss of even one life. And because war is wrong, we must do whatever we can to end conscription everywhere. We firmly maintain that no cause, however just, is rationale enough to force a man to fight to kill.

2. Using Noun Clauses as Subjects

In this conversation, complete the answers by forming noun clauses based on the questions.

A: What did the boss tell Charlie?

B: ___*What the boss told Charlie*___ does not concern me.

1.

A: Who talked to the boss about Charlie?

B: _____ is none of my business.

2.

A: Where is Charlie now?

B: _____ is not my concern.

3.

A: When is Charlie going to be arrested?

B: _____ does not interest me.

4.

A: When was the money stolen?

B: _____ doesn't matter at this point.

5.

A: What will happen to Charlie?

B: _____ is no concern of mine.

6.

A: I wonder whether or not Charlie is a thief.

B: I don't. _____ won't change the world.

7.

A: It's amazing! We have a big-time embezzler in our company!

B: The fact that _____ hasn't been established yet.

8.

A: I don't understand. What do you think about this news?

B: I thought you understood by now. _____ is that it's not right to gossip.

9.

3. Using Noun Clauses as Objects

Beth Crier, a reporter on a high school newspaper, has interviewed Mr. Fred Evans, the director of sports at her school. Complete his answers by forming noun clauses based on the questions. Introduce each clause with one of the following words: **what, where, that, whatever, whoever.**

Crier: Are sports important to the development of young people?

Evans: Yes, anyone involved with young people and sports can tell you ___*that sports are*___

1.
___*important to the development of young people*___.

(continued on next page)

Crier: In that case, do you think a school's curriculum should include a strong sports program?

Evans: Definitely. I'm firmly convinced _____
2.

_____.

Crier: What can students do to become part of a team?

Evans: I'm often asked _____
3.

_____. The first step, of course, is to come and try out for the team.

Crier: I've heard that in order to be on a team students don't have to have a lot of talent. Is this true?

Can anyone who is interested in a sport and tries hard be on a team?

Evans: Absolutely. There's a place on a team for _____
4.

_____.

Crier: Is training necessary?

Evans: Yes. And prospective team members should be prepared to do _____
5.

_____.

Crier: Is the training difficult?

Evans: Sometimes it can be. But anyone who is really committed to a team doesn't care _____
6.

_____.

Crier: Tell me how it works for an individual student on the team. What does he or she have to do?

Where does he or she belong?

Evans: It's hard to give a general answer to those questions. But I can assure you that before long

each student on a team knows _____
7.

and _____.
8.

Crier: What does it feel like to be a team player?

Evans: The players don't usually talk about _____,
9.

_____, but it's obvious that they feel good about themselves.

4.   Editing

Read the following passage. Find and correct the nine errors in the use of noun clauses.

Among conscientious objectors are the Quakers, also known as the Religious Society of Friends. The Quaker religion originated in seventeenth-century England with George Fox, who believed ~~what~~ *that* a person needs no spiritual intermediary. He sought to know how does a person find understanding and guidance and concluded that is it through an "inward light," supplied by the Holy Spirit. The early Quakers refused to attend the Church of England services or to pay tithes to the church. They questioned what were the real values in life, and they were frugal and plain in their dress and speech. In those times, whomever opposed the customs of the established church was persecuted. Thus, the Quakers met with fines, confiscation of property, and even imprisonment. Some emigrated to Asia and Africa, but particularly to America, where they found refuge in Rhode Island and in Pennsylvania, a colony established in 1682 by William Penn, who was himself a Quaker.

Quakers do not believe in taking part in war because they feel that war it causes spiritual damage through hatred. Most Quakers refuse to serve in the military, although individuals can follow whatever convictions do they personally hold. Because their resistance is based on religious and humanitarian convictions, the U.S. and British governments have allowed them to substitute nonmilitary service for that would normally be a military service requirement.

Quaker meetings are periods of silent meditation, where members speak if they are urged by the spirit. Quakers are active in education and social welfare. They believe society should treat all its citizens as equals. The American Friends Service Committee organizes relief and service projects for whatever in the world help is needed.

5. Personalization

Have you ever pondered the meaning of life? Describe some of the things you have thought about. Include some of the partial sentences in the box.

I've often wondered what life . . .

I've sometimes thought that . . .

That a higher force exists seems . . .

I really don't understand how . . .

What life's meaning is seems . . .

I have sometimes asked whether it . . .

Nobody has been able to tell me if there . . .

Perhaps one day I will comprehend why . . .

I am convinced that . . .

_____

_____

_____

_____

_____

_____

_____

_____

_____

_____

_____

_____

_____

_____

_____

_____

Underline the ten noun clauses that are used as adjective complements or subject complements. Label the clauses as adjective complement or subject complement.

U N I T

19

Complementation

THE SUNDAY MAGAZINE

By now, much has been made of gender differences in language. Partly because of the recent publication of several books and articles on the subject, it appears clear to many people <u>that men</u> *adjective complement* <u>speak more directly than women do</u> and, in addition, that a direct way of speaking is more effective than an indirect way of speaking. It is also a sign of power and self-confidence. ("Type this letter" or "Could you please type this letter" are examples of direct ways of speaking. In contrast, "This letter needs to be typed right away" is an example of an indirect way of conveying the same message.)

However, Dr. Deborah Tannen, a linguist who is an expert in speech patterns, questions these commonly held beliefs. "I challenge the assumption that talking in an indirect way necessarily reveals powerlessness, lack of self-confidence, or anything else about the character of the speaker," she says in an article in the *New York Times.* Moreover, a key finding of hers is that the degree of directness of speech varies greatly among cultures. Finally, according to Tannen, it is also likely that both women and men are indirect. They are often just indirect in different ways, she says.

Addressing the question of effectiveness in giving commands, she does not think it is true that

(continued on next page)

directness always works best. On the contrary, indirectness is often appropriate and successful. She cites examples from the army and from business offices, in which the boss, or the higher-ranking person, effectively uses very indirectly stated orders. For instance, the high-ranking person says: "It's cold in here." These words are really an indirect order; that is, the person's expectation is that one of the subordinates will close the window right away. Or the high-ranking person says, "I wonder whether there is information available on this subject." When these words are spoken, it is advisable that the subordinate quickly find and present the information. Because everybody understands who is in charge, the indirect way of speaking works well.

It should appear obvious, then, that more than the choice of vocabulary and tone of voice determine whether a command is successful. Indeed, a very important consideration is that the status of the speaker and the listener be mutually understood and that both people interact in accordance with the unwritten rules of this understanding. Both women and men can issue effective commands, and both indirect and direct ways of speaking can be effective.

2. Writing Adjective, Subject, and Verb Complements

Complete the following letter by filling in blanks with the indicated words to form appropriate adjective, subject, and verb complements. Include the word **that**. *Write noun clauses, although a few of the sentences could also be completed in other ways.*

Dear Ricardo,

I got your letter. You are really direct, and you are also right. It's true *that I have to shape up*.
1. (I / have to / shape up)

I know it's essential _____. Yet it also seems clear _____.
2. (I / forget / about Lisa)   3. (this / be / much easier said than done)

The problem is _____. I'm sure that you're right when you say that somebody
4. (I / not / can / forget / about her)

new might make me forget. But the big difficulty with this is _____. I'm
5. (I / not / be / receptive to meeting people)

going to try, though. My goal now is _____.
6. (I / get / my life in order)

And you, Ricardo—what's going to happen to you? You lost another job! It's absolutely

necessary _____, *It's obvious* _____.
       7. (you / be / responsible on the job)   8. (you / have / always / be / too casual about your work)

It's vital _____, *if you get one. I recommend* _____.
       9. (you / keep / the next job / you / get)   10. (you / adopt / a better attitude)

And I strongly suggest _____.
       11. (you / not / invest / any more money in bad deals)

      With that advice, I'm signing off.

            Marco

3.   Using Noun Clauses as Adjective Complements

Read the following proverbs. Write paraphrases of the proverbs by using the cues to write sentences in the form **It is** + *adjective* + *noun clause with* **that.** *Then match the paraphrases to the proverbs by putting the correct letter after each paraphrase.*

A. All work and no play makes Jack a dull boy.

B. A stitch in time saves nine.

C. Rome wasn't built in a day.

D. The early bird gets the worm.

E. Children should be seen and not heard.

F. People who live in glass houses shouldn't throw stones.

G. A bird in the hand is worth two in the bush.

H. Don't put the cart before the horse.

I. Don't cry over spilt milk.

J. There's no use putting a lock on the barn door after the horse has been stolen.

1.   *E. It is advisable that children be seen and not heard.*
          advisable / children / be / see / and not / hear

2. _____
          necessary / time/be / take / to do a job right

3. _____
          advisable / you / not criticize / others because you have faults, too

4. _____
          essential / things / be / do / in the right order

5. _____
          advisable / problems / be / take care of / before they get worse

6. _____
          important / you / not be upset / over what already happened

(continued on next page)

7. _____
   desirable / a person / stick / with what he or she already has rather than going after other things

8. _____
   vital / a person / enjoy life / as well as / work

9. _____
   essential / a person / get / an early start to beat the competition

10. _____
   necessary / precautions / be / take / *before* there is trouble.

4. Editing

Read the following essay. Find and correct the eight errors related to noun clauses.
Several noun clauses are used correctly.

Would you believe that listening to the music of Mozart actually makes you smarter?

According to a study, ^*it* is true that Mozart's music has this effect! Recently, researchers at the University

of California, Irvine, found that the IQ scores of college students went up nine points after the students

had been listening to Mozart for ten minutes. In another experiment, it appeared that Mozart's music

helped students to solve spatial puzzles involving cutout shapes. The fact it is that students who

listened to Mozart performed better than those who listened to another composer's music.

These research findings lead to some fascinating speculations. If it is clear that experiencing

Mozart raise the level of intelligence, shouldn't we all have his music on at every moment? Shouldn't

we be using our Walkmans at the office, playing tapes of Mozart's music while we work?

That a schoolchild studying multiplication tables should play Mozart in the background it

seems clear. The child should not listen to Sibelius or Bach, and certainly should not listen to rock or

rap. It should be obvious to the parents because that they must fill the house with Mozart's music and

insist that the child listen to Mozart and only Mozart when studying. What's more, parents should

demand the child listen to Mozart on a headset while playing competitive sports. Of course, the

problem is that as soon as parents begin to insist that something is done in a certain way, they will

meet strong resistance from their children.

Another obvious problem is it that much more research must be done before we can believe

that Mozart's music can actually make you smarter. Meanwhile, though, I personally am willing to try

anything, especially the pleasant task of immersing myself in beautiful music! *

* Based on "Classic View," by Alex Ross, *The New York Times,* August 28, 1994.

5. Personalization

What do you think is necessary to improve the quality of education in today's world? Answer this question in a short essay. Include some of the phrases in the box.

A main problem in education is the fact that . . .

A main problem in our schools is that . . .

It is known that . . .

That schools should . . . is clear.

That students need . . . is obvious.

It is absolutely essential that . . .

It is also desirable that . . .

I would recommend that . . .

We must insist that . . .

The result of making changes like these will be that . . .

UNIT

20

Unreal Conditionals and Other Ways to Express Unreality

1. Identifying Unreal Conditionals

Read the following. Underline the unreal conditionals. Do not underline real conditionals.

The dictionary defines "chocoholic" as a person who has a near obsession for chocolate. The world is full of chocoholics. Yet, <u>if it hadn't been for an unusual sequence of events, these people would probably never have tasted chocolate</u>.

• •

Until the Spanish explorers brought chocolate back from the New World, it was totally unknown in Europe. Arriving in Mexico in the early 1500s, Hernán Cortés discovered that the Indians there drank a delicious, dark, frothy beverage called *chocolatl,* brewed from the beans of the native cacao plant. Cacao beans were so highly valued in the area that they were used as currency. In the marketplace of Chichén Itzá, a center of Mayan Indian civilization, four beans, would buy a pumpkin and 100 would buy a slave. The Indians of Mexico evidently had chocoholics as well as chocolate. Whenever the Aztec Indian king Montezuma didn't drink his 50 pitchers of *chocolatl* a day, it is said, he would feel a strong physical need for it.

It's a good thing for the chocolate lovers of the world that Cortés actually met Montezuma. If he hadn't, the delicious substance might never have crossed the ocean to Spain. Chocolate was popular in Spain for a century before the news of its divine taste and reputed medicinal and psychological powers spread to other European countries. In mid-seventeenth-century London, chocolate houses, like coffee houses, sprang up; only the aristocrats could enjoy the drink, however, because of its high cost. If it hadn't been so expensive, the masses could have enjoyed it much sooner.

Theobromine, a substance similar to caffeine, is found in chocolate, which explains why people felt energized after drinking chocolate. Doctors of the era reported that chocolate was an effective medicine, imparting energy, among other things. If people wanted to feel stronger fast, they could imbibe some of the drink.

Chocolate was primarily a beverage until the 1800s, when a Swiss chocolatier combined chocolate with milk solids. If this chocolatier hadn't, we would not have the wide range of candies and candy bars that we have today. If he hadn't, Switzerland and the Netherlands would not have become the great producers of quality chocolates that they are. Last but not least, if he hadn't, we would not have chocolate cakes or chocolate chip cookies.

Today, 75 percent of the cacao comes from Africa, and the rest comes from Central America, Ecuador, and Brazil. Chocolate is consumed all over the world, but particularly in Western Europe and in the United States. Clearly, if there were not such a well-developed world trade, chocolate lovers would not be able to indulge themselves so easily.

But, chocolate does have some bad effects. It contains a lot of fats and sugar, so if people eat too much, they can develop or worsen conditions such as hardening of the arteries or diabetes. Doctors and dentists have been telling patients for a long time that if their fat and sugar intake were lower, they would be healthier. Such warnings do not do much to inhibit chocoholics. Says one chocoholic, "Quite frankly, if I had a day without chocolate, it would be like a day without sunshine." *

* Information taken from Richard B. Manchester, *Amazing Facts,* (New York: Bristol Park Books, 1991).

2. Relating Unreal Conditions to Real Conditions

The following sentences express unreal conditions. After these sentences, write sentences that express what the real conditions are.

1. If chocolate weren't so delicious, people wouldn't crave it.

   Chocolate ____is delicious____.

   People ____crave it____.

2. If chocolate hadn't been brought back to Europe by the Spanish explorers, it might not be popular today.

   Chocolate _____.

   It _____.

(continued on next page)

3. People would be healthy if they didn't eat a lot of chocolate and other foods containing fat and

sugar.

People _____.

They _____.

4. If people ate a balanced diet, they would be well nourished.

People _____.

They _____.

5. Some people wish that they had enough willpower to refuse junk food.

Some people don't _____.

6. People on diets often wish, for example, that they hadn't consumed 4,000 calories at the last meal

that they ate.

Some people on diets actually _____.

7. Gourmands are people who eat greedily, as though there were no tomorrow.

There really _____.

8. If only dieting were easy!

Dieting _____.

| 3. | **Expressing Conditions in the Present Time** |

Complete Jane's diary. In the first four paragraphs, fill in the blanks with appropriate clauses expressing unreal conditions *in the present time. Use* **would** *in conditional sentences. In the last paragraph, fill in the blanks with clauses expressing* possible conditions *in the present time.*

Dear Diary,

I have just come from Cousin Hattie's annual Thanksgiving dinner, where once again

I had to endure all the questions from family members about why I am not married.

This really upsets me! I'm not married because I choose not to be. If

I chose to be married, I would be married. Actually, part of the reason is that I never meet
　　　1. (I / choose / be married / I / be married)

anyone I really like. Perhaps, if_____.
　　　　　　　　　　　　2. (I / meet / the right man / I / have a different feeling about it)

As usual, everyone was worried about me, thinking that I'm lonely. If

_____. But I do have a lot of friends, so I'm fine.
        3. (I / not have / a lot of friends / I / be lonely)

Maybe if _____. But I like my job a lot.
        4. (I / not like / my job / I / be unhappy)

I'm tired of being nagged about the subject of marriage all the time. I really wish

_____. My family sometimes treats me as though
    5. (people / leave / me alone)

_____ for choosing to remain single. But I am not weird.
    6. (I / be / a / weird person)

Actually, I wouldn't mind having a partner in life. If only

_____! Not to sound greedy, but sometimes I wish
    7. (I / can / meet / the perfect man tomorrow)

_____ —a successful career, travel, an active social
    8. (I / have / it all)

life, and a husband and children. I think I could manage it.

    Actually, I do hope _____ really nice. But where? I know! I'll
                  9. (I / meet / somebody)

try Warm Hearts. From what I've heard, it seems as if _____.
                                      10. (that / be / an excellent matchmaking service)

If only _____! Then what will my family nag
        11. (they / introduce / me to someone perfect)

me about?

---

4.   Expressing Conditionals in the Past Time

*Complete the letter by filling in the blanks to express unreal conditions in the
past time. Use the indicated words, and use* **would** *in the result clauses of
conditional sentences.*

Dear Ricardo,

    Well, all's well that ends well, as Shakespeare said. Even though a lot of bad things happened to

me, my year here in the United States has actually been pretty good. First, and most important, I

met Suzie. It's a good thing, because if I ____*hadn't met*____ Suzie, I would have been suffering
                                1. (meet / not)

over Lisa for a really long time. For that matter, it's a good thing that I had the automobile accident;

if I hadn't crashed into that little blue Mazda, I _____ its driver, who turned out
                                  2. (never / meet)

(continued on next page)

to be Suzie. Suzie has taken over my life, and it's so much better now. Suzie influenced me to drop my

history course. I didn't know that it was possible to drop courses. If I hadn't dropped the course, I

_____ it for sure. I wish that I _____ so much time taking it; I
   3. (fail)   4. (not / waste)

should have dropped it sooner. Another thing that's much better since I met Suzie: the food. Yes,

Suzie is a wonderful cook. If I had known Suzie earlier, I _____ all those terrible
                                      5. (not / have to eat)

meals at the beginning of the semester. If I had known Suzie earlier, I _____
                                    6. (know)

where to get an apartment and where to shop. If I had known Suzie earlier, I _____
                                    7. (not / be)

as lonesome and homesick as I was at the beginning, and I certainly _____ over
                                    8. (not / suffer)

Lisa like a stupid, lovesick puppy the way that I did. If only I _____ her when
                                  9. (meet)

I first came here!

I'm glad that you're OK now, too, Ricardo. It's too bad that things didn't work out at the

hotel. Maybe if you _____ at the desk so often at that job, you wouldn't have
                 10. (not / fall asleep)

gotten fired. But as my mother always says, "Things work out for the best," and your present job

making movies sounds glamorous. Just think, if you hadn't gotten fired, you _____
                                    11. (not / be able to)

take the job with the movie producer last spring. And, taking classes at night and working during the

day is a good idea. Who knows? Maybe you'll even become a movie star. Of course, you might become

very snobbish as a movie star and act as though you _____ me or anybody
                                  12. (never / meet)

else from our childhood. But I think that won't happen.

Actually, I wish that the bad stuff this year _____, but as I said,
                                13. (not / happen)

everything's turning out OK. You have a great and glamorous new job, you're paying off your

debts and you have a future. I will finish school here, and I have a wonderful new girlfriend. If we

_____ some of the mistakes we did, these good things _____
  14. (not / make)   15. (pass)

us by. What you should do is visit me here in the United States when you are between movies, or

maybe when you come to the United States "on location."

See you soon, I hope.

Marco

5. Editing

Read the following letter. Find and correct the nine errors in the forms of the verbs in the conditional and related sentences.

Dear Elinor,

I am writing because I want to talk to you about a woman I met though Warm Hearts, a matchmaking service here in Beautiville. Her name is Jane, and I'd like to build a relationship with her. The trouble is that I'm too shy. Oh, I wish I ~~didn't be~~ *weren't* so shy! If I weren't so shy, I would called her up to invite her out to dinner. It's a good thing that I signed up with Warm Hearts. If I hadn't, I would never had met such a wonderful girl, because as you know, I just can't bring myself to call anyone for a date.

Anyway, Jane is beautiful and smart and very nice. I think I am falling in love with her, and I haven't even spent time with her. We've only talked on the phone. I wish we have already been out together a hundred times. I feel as though I knew her all my life. If you talked to her, you would liked her, too, I know.

Elinor, here's my question. You know I have always been a shy man. If I actually gathered enough courage to ask her out, what did she say? I think she'd say yes, because, after all, she joined the dating service and she does spend time with me on the phone. It isn't as though we are kids, either. She's 40, just a few years younger than I am. So, Elinor, what do you think I should do?

I hope that you answered me soon.

Your brother Gus

6. Personalization

How would you evaluate the quality of your life at this point? Have you made decisions which turned out well? Write a short essay about your life now and about how decisions you made have influenced your life. Finish some of the sentences in the box.

> The best decision I have made in my life was . . .
>
> If I had made the opposite decision, . . .
>
> On the other hand, a bad decision was . . .
>
> I wish I . . .
>
> If I . . .
>
> There are many aspects of my present situation that I wouldn't change. For example, I wouldn't change . . .
>
> If I were to change . . .
>
> My life now is too . . .
>
> I wish my life . . .
>
> If my life . . .
>
> I hope . . .

_____

_____

_____

_____

_____

_____

_____

_____

_____

_____

_____

U N I T

21

Inverted
and Implied
Conditionals;
Subjunctive in
Noun Clauses
▼

1. Identifying Inverted and Implied Conditionals and Subjunctives in Noun Clauses

In the following article,* look for inverted and implied conditionals and subjunctives in noun clauses. Underline clauses containing an inverted conditional (do not underline other conditional clauses), words introducing implied conditionals, and verbs in subjunctive form in noun clauses.

It is difficult to imagine what life would be like today <u>had the can opener not been invented</u>. Without the simple little tool that we take for granted, how would we open cans? It is essential that we have the can opener to gain the enormous advantages in time, variety of foods, and, most of all, convenience that the use of canned goods gives us. What if we had no way of preserving the foods we are so accustomed to buying in cans today? We would not be eating the tuna, canned hams, or out-of-season peas and peaches that are so much a part of our lifestyle. Without canned tuna, the popular tuna sandwich wouldn't exist.

SCIENCE JOURNAL

Interestingly, metal cans to preserve food had been in existence for a full fifty years before a device similar to the can opener we know today was invented. Developed in England in 1810, the first "tin canisters" were actually made of iron and sometimes heavier than the food they contained. British soldiers in the War of 1812 opened canned rations with bayonets, knives, or even rifles. On an Arctic expedition in 1824, British explorer Sir William Parry took along a can of veal, the instructions of which read: "Cut round on the top with a chisel and hammer"; empty, the can weighed more than a pound. By the 1850s, cans were made of a lighter metal and had a rim around the top. Around this time, Ezra J. Warner of Waterbury, Connecticut, devised a "can opener." This opener was part bayonet and part sickle; if not used correctly, it could be lethal. Had the U.S. military not adopted this primitive can opener in the Civil War, surely the unwieldy invention would soon have become extinct.

But, as the saying has it, necessity is the mother of invention. In 1870, William J. Lyman patented a device that was revolutionary in concept and design: it had a cutting wheel that rolled around the rim of the can. Because of the ease with which cans could now be opened, by 1895 canned goods were a familiar sight on grocery store shelves. In 1925 a serrated rotation wheel was added, and in 1931 the electric can opener was introduced.

The evolution of this important invention did not occur overnight. How fortunate we are that lightweight cans and easy-to-use can openers were invented; otherwise, we would not have the convenience and variety in foods that we have.

* Based on Charles Panati, *Extraordinary Origins of Everyday Things,* (Perennial Library, Harper & Row, 1987, Revised 1989).

2.   Using the Subjunctive in Noun Clauses

*In the following material providing advice to travelers, incorporate each sentence
in parentheses into the next sentence as a noun clause.*

1. (A driver must keep to the right-hand side of the road.)

   In the United States and many European countries, it is essential *that a driver keep* *to the right-hand side of the road*.

2. (He or she has to drive on the left.)

   In Japan and England, however, it is mandatory _____
   _____.

3. (People should remove their shoes before going inside a house.)

   In some places, such as Japan and Saudi Arabia, it is important _____
   _____.

4. (People should keep their shoes on.)

   In other places, it is expected _____
   _____.

5. (People must not eat pork products.)

   In some places, religious laws demand _____
   _____.

6. (Pork products must be avoided.)

   This is because in olden times, the hot weather required _____
   _____, because of the strong possibility of food contamination.

7. (A sick person should take vitamin C.)

   In some places, doctors recommend _____
   _____.

8. (A sick person should have a lot of homemade chicken soup.)

   In other places, they advise _____
   _____.

9. (A waiter should be summoned by whistling.)

   In some places, it is suggested _____
   _____.

(continued on next page)

10. (A waiter must not be summoned by whistling.)

In other places, it is recommended _____

_____, because this would be considered exceedingly rude.

11. (A traveler ought to learn about customs in various places.)

Logic suggests _____

_____.

3. Using Inverted and Implied Conditionals in the Past Time

*Complete the following answers to questions in an American history examination
by filling in the blanks with the appropriate conditional forms of the verbs
indicated. Use* **would** *in result clauses unless another auxiliary is indicated.*

1. As everyone knows, Columbus discovered the New World quite accidentally while searching

   for a shorter route to India. Had he ___*not been searching*___ for that shorter route to India, he
   (not / be searching)

   ___*would not have discovered*___ the New World.
   (not / discover)

2. The American colonists formally gained their independence from England in 1783. Had

   the Americans _____ their independence from England, America
   (not / gain)

   _____ a British colony.
   (remain)

3. In the American Civil War, fought from 1861 to 1865, the North had greater resources and

   finally won the war. Without these resources, the North _____ the Civil War.
   (might / not / win)

4. The railroads were very important to the development of the American West and

   directly contributed to the growth of California. Without the railroads, California

   _____ as quickly as it did.
   (not / grow)

5. During its history, America has attracted and welcomed people from many different

   cultures. Had America _____ these differing peoples, the country
   (reject)

   _____ the multicultural nation that it is today.
   (not / become)

6. Women won the right to vote in the United States in 1920. Had women _____
   (not / win)

   that right in 1920, it is probable that they _____ it before now in any case.
   (gain)

7. In 1955, Jonas Salk, an American physician, developed a vaccine to prevent polio. It is indeed fortunate that he developed this vaccine; if not, many more people _____ of (die) polio in the last forty years.

8. John F. Kennedy was assassinated in November 1963. Had he _____, he (live) probably _____ two terms as president of the United States. (serve)

4. Writing Conditionals

For each of the following sentences, write a corresponding conditional sentence that expresses the opposite situation. Begin the sentence with the phrase given and include **would** *or* **wouldn't**.

How do major inventions change our lives? Imagine life over the centuries as it has been changed by various inventions.

1. We have can openers, with which we are able to open cans. Without can openers, *we wouldn't* _____ *be able to open cans* _____.

2. By using forks and chopsticks, we don't have to use our fingers to eat. Without forks and chopsticks, _____.

3. Because electricity was discovered, we have electric lights, movies, television, and computers. Had electricity _____.

4. Jet planes did not exist in the last century; people did not travel extensively then. Had jet planes _____.

5. Television is available throughout the world; as a result, fashions, music, and basic values are very similar in many places. Were television _____.

6. Because computers were developed, businesses are able to obtain the data they need to function in today's competitive world. Had computers _____.

7. With computers, the general public has easy access to extensive knowledge. Without computers, _____.

5. Editing

Read the following passage. Find and correct the twelve errors in the forms of conditionals and subjunctives. Several of the conditional and subjunctive sentences are correct.

I have often fantasized about the perfect world. It would be perfect not only for my family and me, but for everyone.

First of all, ~~we were~~ *were we* living in a perfect world, there would be food for everyone. No one would be starving or without regular sources of food. Second, in this perfect world, everything would be clean and free of pollution. With clean air and toxin-free water, humans, animals, and plants would stayed healthy. Third, all diseases would be conquered; we will be free of cancer, AIDS, and heart disease. Without those diseases, people could lived longer and be free from terrible suffering. If had scientists already discovered a cure for these diseases, we could now be anticipating a much longer life span. Fourth, were the world in perfect condition, there will be no crime. Societal and psychological factors would not breed the crime that they do. And last, there would be no wars. All countries and all peoples would live together, harmoniously as one.

While these goals may appear unrealistic, it would be wise not to abandon them. Had statesmen abandoned the idea of one world, we don't have the United Nations today. Had scientists given up their search for cures, we will not have found the means to conquer polio, tuberculosis, some types of pneumonia, and many bacteria-caused diseases. Had civic-minded individuals been less tenacious, we did not have cleaned up the cities and waters and air as much as we have. Had we not learned and taught better methods of agriculture and food distribution, many more people would be starving today.

What if it were required by law that all of the *haves*—those people who *have* a decent life and more than enough material things—made concrete contributions to a perfect world? Local governments would require that citizens gave a specified amount of time or money each year to a recognized community project. Would such a program work? It could and should; otherwise, we would have to give up on making appreciable progress toward a better, if not perfect, world. It is absolutely essential that hope is expressed not only in theory, but also tangibly in order to improve the quality of all life on earth.

6.   Personalization

What was the most serious problem you faced and how did you deal with it? How would you deal with a similar problem today? Write a short essay. Include some of the phrases in the box.

One of the most serious problems I faced was . . .

Had I known at the time that . . .

It was essential that I . . .

Without a lot of luck at that time, I . . .

It's indeed fortunate that this happened. What if . . .

Were a similar problem to arise now, I would . . .

Were a similiar problem to arise, I might try to solve it in the same way. If so, . . . Otherwise, . . .

Everyone faces problems like mine. Life demands that we . . .

_____

_____

_____

_____

_____

_____

_____

_____

_____

_____

_____

_____

_____

_____

_____

_____

_____

Answer Key

Note: In this answer key, where the contracted form is given, the full form is also correct, and where the full form is given, the contracted form is also correct.

PART I: The Verb Phrase: Selected Topics

Tense and Time

1.

2. picture **3.** arrived **4.** began **5.** had begun **6.** have been arriving **7.** establish **8.** came **9.** have sprung up **10.** used to be **11.** have become **12.** doesn't exist **13.** would assimilate **14.** has occurred **15.** will be **16.** will be speaking **17.** will be cooking **18.** will have become

2.

2. was **3.** learned **4.** had been working **5.** came **6.** hadn't passed **7.** was studying **8.** worked **9.** had passed **10.** had established **11.** has been practicing **12.** has gained **13.** are having **14.** has been **15.** got **16.** owns **17.** operates **18.** had been taking **19.** got **20.** runs **21.** finds **22.** is going to set up **23.** have been having **24.** got **25.** have been working **26.** will be **27.** will be working **28.** will have established **29.** arrived **30.** had expected **31.** die **32.** will have lived

3.

2. will be/is going to be **3.** gives **4.** will win/is going to win **5.** will receive/is going to receive **6.** joins **7.** will be/is going to be **8.** does **9.** goes **10.** will have/is going to have **11.** enters **12.** will get/is going to get **13.** will have/are going to have **14.** get **15.** will we all be doing **16.** will have been working **17.** get **18.** will have/are going to have

4.

2. B **3.** D **4.** A **5.** A **6.** B **7.** B **8.** B **9.** C **10.** D **11.** A **12.** B

5.

2. are going to hear/will hear/hear/will be hearing/are hearing **3.** used to be/was **4.** has telephoned **5.** left **6.** told **7.** testified **8.** used to steal/would steal/stole **9.** said **10.** had gone/went **11.** had been playing **12.** stopped **13.** was hurting **14.** found **15.** had seen/saw **16.** were talking **17.** went **18.** have been waiting **19.** is saying **20.** seems **21.** has requested **22.** will be watching/are going to be watching **23.** will have learned

6.

have begun → began   had given → give/have given   wrote → was writing   has knocked → knocked   has been → was   has been → was/would be   is caring → cares   am thinking → think   is raining → rains   are being → are   am not understanding → don't understand   has written → wrote   hadn't sent → didn't send   will be → would be   hadn't been → hasn't been   didn't meet → haven't met   hadn't been having → haven't been having   have finished → will have finished   I'll work → I'll be working

7.

(Answers will vary.)

Certainty and Necessity (Modals)

1.

2. should **3.** doesn't have to **4.** needn't **5.** have to **6.** must **7.** should **8.** should **9.** had better

2.

2. can't **3.** could **4.** must **5.** could **6.** couldn't **7.** must **8.** couldn't have

3.

2. should have stayed 3. might have gone 4. must have had to 5. was supposed to call 6. was to telephone 7. may have forgotten 8. couldn't have been 9. must have been

4.

2. C 3. D 4. B 5. D 6. D 7. C 8. B 9. B 10. C

5.

2. must make/have got to make/have to make 3. could cut/might cut 4. could cut/might cut 5. should eliminate/ought to eliminate 6. have to 7. could do/might do 8. must make/have got to make/have to make 9. should invest/ought to invest 10. must make/has got to make/has to make 11. must earn/has got to earn/has to earn 12. must get/has got to get/has to get 13. may need/might need 14. may find/might find/could find 15. should become/ought to become

6.

have apologize → have to apologize   shouldn't had had → shouldn't have had   were suppose → were supposed   must have upsetting → must have upset   couldn't had been → couldn't have been   I've got find → I've got to find   should takes → should take   should to find → should find   could to do → could do   could have pick → could pick   might have offer → might offer   could to do → could do   might been → might be   You've to be → You have to be   has to → have to   must to → must   used to being → used to be

7.

(Answers will vary.)

UNIT 3 Contrast and Emphasis (Auxiliaries)

1.

2. do want 3. did become 4. did clean up 5. do intend 6. do have to 7. do communicate

2.

2. did begin 3. does express 4. did agree 5. does help 6. did speak 7. is 8. is 9. is going to give 10. do feel encouraged 11. does have 12. is going to happen

3.

2. did survive 3. is 4. do eat 5. do vote 6. do know how 7. was 8. do understand 9. does have

4.

does relates → does relate   did believed → did believe   is represent → does represent   did became → did become   did spilled → did spill   does remain →do remain

5.

(Answers will vary.)

PART II: The Noun Phrase: Selected Topics

UNIT 4 Non-Count Nouns: Count and Non-Count Use

1.

1. study NC 2. breadth NC, thought NC, endeavor NC 3. languages C, dialects C, literatures C 4. thoughts C, language NC 5. time NC, language NC 6. space NC, communication NC

2.

transportation education crime violence weather housing accessibility hiking skiing sailing enjoyment nature safety crime violence availability water air employment growth living proximity

3.

2. a piece of 3. a game of 4. a game of 5. a glass of 6. a slice of/a piece of 7. a serving of 8. a piece of/a slice of/a serving of 9. a slice of/a piece of/a serving of 10. a glass of 11. a piece of 12. a branch of 13. a clap of 14. a flash of 15. a piece of 16. a period of

4.

2. a partner **3.** integrity **4.** work **5.** great fun **6.** love
7. practicality **8.** a compatible companion **9.** warmth
10. a career **11.** a job **12.** A good salary **13.** respect

5.

2. Production **3.** ancient history **4.** milk **5.** A favorite dish
6. overcooked rice **7.** snow **8.** a symbol **9.** wealth **10.** ice
11. cream **12.** a way **13.** salt **14.** the ices **15.** music
16. a stick **17.** happiness

6.

history → the history   smokes → smoke
communications → communication   a clay → clay
peoples → people   abstraction → abstractions
alphabet → alphabets   knowledges → knowledge
skill → skills   a literacy → literacy   arithmetics →
arithmetic   informations → information   literacies →
literacy

7.

(Answers will vary.)

UNIT 5 — Definite and Indefinite Articles

1.

2. a **3.** a **4.** The **5.** the **6.** the **7.** an **8.** a **9.** the **10.** a
11. the **12.** the **13.** the **14.** The **15.** 0 **16.** the **17.** a **18.** a
19. 0 **20.** a **21.** The **22.** the **23.** a **24.** the **25.** 0 **26.** 0 **27.** 0
28. 0 **29.** the **30.** 0 **31.** 0 **32.** the

2.

2. the **3.** 0 **4.** 0 **5.** the **6.** 0 **7.** the **8.** 0 **9.** 0 **10.** 0 **11.** 0
12. 0 **13.** A **14.** a **15.** a **16.** A **17.** 0 **18.** 0

3.

2. the **3.** the **4.** the **5.** 0 **6.** the **7.** the **8.** 0 **9.** 0 **10.** the
11. 0 **12.** 0 **13.** the **14.** 0 **15.** the **16.** 0 **17.** the **18.** the
19. the

4.

2. an **3.** the **4.** the **5.** an **6.** a **7.** The **8.** a **9.** 0 **10.** 0
11. The **12.** 0 **13.** 0 **14.** The **15.** 0 **16.** the **17.** a **18.** the
19. the **20.** the **21.** a **22.** 0 **23.** 0 **24.** 0 **25.** 0 **26.** the
27. the **28.** 0

5.

2. the **3.** 0 **4.** 0 **5.** the **6.** the **7.** 0 **8.** 0 **9.** 0 **10.** the **11.** 0
12. 0 **13.** the **14.** The **15.** the **16.** 0 **17.** 0 **18.** 0 **19.** the
20. the **21.** the **22.** the **23.** the **24.** 0 **25.** the **26.** the
27. the **28.** the **29.** the **30.** the **31.** the **32.** the **33.** the
34. the **35.** The **36.** a **37.** the **38.** the **39.** the **40.** the
41. the **42.** the **43.** the **44.** the **45.** the **46.** a **47.** 0 **48.** 0
49. 0 **50.** 0 **51.** a **52.** the **53.** a **54.** 0

6.

zoo → the zoo   the healthy → healthy   a satisfaction →
the satisfaction   male → a male   A lion → The lion   the
schoolchildren → schoolchildren   Arabian kind → the
Arabian kind   Bactrian kind → The Bactrian kind
Chimpanzees → The chimpanzees   human family → a
human family   the arguments → arguments   most
popular animal → the most popular animal   zoo → the
zoo   most expensive → the most expensive   the show →
a show   a visitors → visitors   an applause → the
applause   a life situation → the life situation   a zoo →
the zoo   well-being → the well-being

7.

(Answers will vary.)

UNIT 6 — Modification of Nouns

1.

2. some bright young **3.** these new spring **4.** many different
international **5.** the first exciting new **6.** his long clean
7. much extra **8.** expensive, fine silk/fine, expensive silk
9. some old Japanese **10.** these simple, classic **11.** elegant
business **12.** a soft, feminine **13.** his wild, brightly colored
14. far-off, tropical South Sea **15.** casual daytime **16.** the
liveliest new **17.** Those hot pink **18.** several brilliant purple
19. long, flowing cotton **20.** any well-known clothes
21. these fabulous new

2.

2. flower gardens **3.** vegetable gardens **4.** work horses
5. show horses **6.** house cats **7.** house guests **8.** guest
house **9.** strawberry jam **10.** blackberry tea **11.** peach pie
12. kitchen table **13.** childhood memories **14.** childhood
dreams **15.** baby sister **16.** summer night

3.

2. one two-hundred-year-old dining room table **3.** eight velvet-covered dining room chairs **4.** two century-old Tiffany lamps **5.** one silver-plated samovar **6.** one leaded crystal chandelier **7.** two (one)-hundred-(and)-fifty-year-old rocking chairs **8.** one hand-woven Persian carpet **9.** one hand-written manuscript **10.** three ivory-inlaid coffee tables **11.** four hand-painted serving dishes **12.** two hand-carved mahogany beds **13.** two (one) hundred-(and)-thirty-year-old, gold-inlaid vases

4.

publishing glamorous world → glamorous publishing world   southwest beautiful Montana → beautiful

southwest Montana   blue, clear skies → clear, blue skies   gray, dirty smog → dirty, gray smog   respiratory mysterious ailment → mysterious respiratory ailment   ten-days siege → ten-day siege   four-rooms apartment → four-room apartment   dreary, jail, cement cell → dreary, cement jail cell   new prized job → prized new job   forty-two-years-old, feverish body → feverish, forty-two-year-old body (two mistakes)   Iron gigantic hammers → Gigantic iron hammers   black lead, huge weights → huge, black lead weights   two-hours rest → two-hour rest   New York unspeakably rude reception → unspeakably rude New York reception   three first weeks → first three weeks

5.

(Answers will vary.)

UNIT 7 Quantifiers

1.

every   certain   some   less   fewer   little   enough   all   No   either   more   a few   most of   much   plenty of   The amount of   a great deal of   neither of   A number of   none of   both   each of   more   many of

2.

2. a few **3.** a great deal of **4.** a little **5.** many **6.** any **7.** a bit of **8.** all **9.** A couple of **10.** every **11.** a bunch of **12.** a couple of **13.** most of **14.** a lot of **15.** a great deal of **16.** a few of **17.** a little

3.

2. less **3.** Many **4.** a great deal of **5.** Many **6.** some **7.** many **8.** few **9.** a lot of **10.** some **11.** a great number of

4.

2. some **3.** number **4.** certain **5.** many **6.** Some **7.** Some **8.** Most of **9.** an amount of **10.** Either **11.** a certain **12.** less

5.

Some of the errors may also be corrected in other ways.
A few people → Few people   either their immediate needs and their future needs → both their immediate needs and their future needs   fewer anxiety → less anxiety   many more money → much more money   every of your assets → all of your assets   the number of information → the amount of information   several advice → some advice   each of the news → all of the news   a few extra money → a little extra money   neither of those → either of those   a great deal of possible scenarios → a great number of possible scenarios   a great number of thought → a great deal of thought

6.

(Answers will vary.)

PART III: Passive Voice

UNIT 8 The Passive: Review and Expansion

1.

will be covered   is designed   have to be accommodated   must be displayed   having . . . built   can be absorbed   is going to be equipped   have . . . washed   will get served   will be . . . run   has been given   is . . . seen   have . . . furnished   may be cleaned   have been advised   can be trapped   have . . . installed   will have been spent

2.

2. will be caressed **3.** laze **4.** savor **5.** will be thrilled **6.** must be seen **7.** must be enjoyed **8.** are spoken **9.** will be delighted **10.** were settled **11.** were enchanted **12.** left **13.** can experience **14.** speak **15.** will be enchanted **16.** was colonized **17.** are not allowed **18.** may be rented **19.** are imported/have been imported

3.

2. was begun **3.** was completely designed **4.** is surrounded
5. be spoiled **6.** are being built **7.** have a garden center put
in **8.** have organic vegetables grown **9.** can be cleaned
10. can easily be maintained **11.** can be replaced **12.** have
been influenced **13.** has to be budgeted **14.** must be spent
15. must be carefully considered **16.** have everything made
17. has been done **18.** will have been completed **19.** will
have been installed

4.

Identifications: 2. had ever had the heads of the tape
player cleaned **3.** had some furniture sent **4.** have it
shortened, have future alterations done **5.** have had it
checked **6.** had had a car sent
New causatives: 2. should have the tapes transferred to
regular cassettes **3.** have your table looked at by an
insurance adjuster **4.** have the bill sent to him **5.** will have
the problem fixed **6.** have your son picked up

5.

2. get my car fixed **3.** got towed **4.** got charged **5.** got
stolen **6.** got dumped **7.** get hired **8.** gets asked **9.** get
fired

6.

1b. They can be toasted easily. **c.** They were introduced to
Mexico by the Spanish. **d.** And before that, they had been
brought to Spain by the Moors. **2a.** Pepitas are ground for
use in sauces. **b.** They also are eaten whole. **c.** Even if they
have been ground, the sauce has a rough texture.
d. Pepitas have been used since pre-Columbian times.

3a. In Mexico, it is made of unsmoked meat and spices.
b. In Spain the meat is smoked. **4a.** Street vendors in
Mexico sell jicama in thick slices that have been sprinkled
with salt, lime juice, and chili powder. **5a.** Avocados are
considered a true delicacy. **b.** If they are hard, they should
be allowed to ripen. **c.** Guacamole is made from avocados.
d. Avocados also are used in salads and as a garnish.
6a. Meat is steamed in little packets of banana leaves.
b. First, they must be softened over a flame. **c.** Then, the
meat and other ingredients are wrapped in them. **7a.** They
are cooked in various ways, including deep-frying and
baking. **b.** Firm green bananas may be substituted.
8a. They can be eaten with any meal. **b.** They are made
from corn or wheat flour. **c.** Frozen tortillas can now be
found in supermarkets. **9a.** Chilies are used to season
many different dishes. **b.** Chili-seasoned foods have been
consumed for more than 8,000 years. **10a.** Corn is used
widely in Mexico. **b.** In Mexican cooking, no part of the
corn is wasted. **c.** The ears, husks, silk, and kernels are
used in different ways. **d.** This was the first plant that was
cultivated in Mexico.

7.

which also known → which is also known   have been
occurred → have occurred   has never found → has never
been found   have been proposing → have been proposed
have proven → have been proven   have frequently been
record → have frequently been recorded   has been
find → has been found   usually are form → usually are
formed   draw by → are drawn by

8.

(Answers will vary.)

Reporting Ideas and Facts with Passives

1.

are believed   is now known   is now understood   are
regarded   are assumed   has been found   had been
considered   was reported   is recommended   are known
are suggested   are considered

2.

2. is believed **3.** was previously thought **4.** is understood
5. is well known **6.** would be perceived **7.** is widely
confirmed **8.** has been well established **9.** are said **10.** has
been considered **11.** can be assumed

3.

2. is believed **3.** is claimed/had previously been thought
4. are reported **5.** is not known **6.** is now assumed **7.** is
also thought **8.** was conjectured **9.** are now believed **10.** is
said **11.** is known **12.** is known **13.** is now thought **14.** can
safely be assumed

4.

believes to go further → is believed to go further   been
recognized → have been recognized   is no longer
consider → is no longer considered   are now considering
→ are now considered   has eliminated → has been
eliminated   now prohibited → is now prohibited   have
made → have been made   is still thinking → is still
thought   hasn't been doing → hasn't been done   is
considering → is considered   has now been establishing
→ has now been established   it also know → is also
known   feels → is felt   is assumes → is assumed   are
regard → are regarded   fined → are fined   jailed → are
jailed   will need → will be needed   not permitted → is
not permitted   have established → have been established
are being educating → are being educated   is conjecturing
→ is conjectured   will been almost eliminated → will
have been almost eliminated

5.

(Answers will vary.)

PART IV: Gerunds and Infinitives

 Gerunds

1.

relieving, building, training, participating, walking, jogging, swimming, lifting, doing, exercising, hiking, bicycling, socializing, Being included, bicycling, learning, Producing, improving

2.

2. not having been **3.** having stopped by **4.** having seen **5.** having met **6.** having telephoned **7.** having become **8.** not having stopped

3.

2. being bothered **3.** Being required **4.** having been chosen **5.** not being fooled **6.** having been selected **7.** being perceived **8.** being cheated **9.** being disturbed **10.** having been solicited

4.

2. Tom is annoyed by Helen's talking on the phone to her boss on weekends. **3.** Helen can't tolerate Tom's being

rude to her/Helen's family. **4.** Tom dislikes Helen's cooking. **5.** Helen is disturbed by Tom's swearing at other drivers. **6.** Helen resents Tom's spending hours in front of the TV. **7.** Tom can't sleep because of Helen's snoring. **8.** I can't stand their fighting all the time when I'm around them. **9.** I really appreciate your always having good advice.

5.

bless → being blessed   Play → Playing   paint → painting   sculpt → sculpting   Collect → Collecting   weave → weaving   pottery make → pottery making   wood carve → wood carving   use → using   make → making   sail → sailing   play → playing   Recognize → Being recognized   express → expressing   find → finding

6.

(Answers will vary.)

 Infinitives

1.

to give and receive   to give   to receive   to be receiving   not to have received   to be included   not to receive   to become hardened   to be rehabilitated   to continue   to have been reached and touched   to be rehabilitated

2.

2. I would go to the Caribbean (in order) to sail, swim, dive, and snorkel. **3.** I would go to Switzerland or Colorado (in order) to ski. **4.** I would go to Egypt (in order) to visit pyramids. **5.** I would go to Japan (in order) to see Mount Fujiyama. **6.** I would go to Kenya (in order) to photograph large wild animals. **7.** I would go to Paris (in order) to shop for original designer clothes. **8.** I would go to Italy (in order) to walk around the ruins of ancient Rome. **9.** I would go to Brazil (in order) to dance the samba and lambada. **10.** I would go to Disneyland (in order to) meet Mickey Mouse and Donald Duck.

3.

2. to dance **3.** to be **4.** to have been **5.** to be remembered/to have been remembered **6.** to reminisce **7.** to cry **8.** to conceal **9.** to love **10.** (to) cherish **11.** to attend

4.

2. to love **3.** to be **4.** to be picked up **5.** (to be) given **6.** to ride **7.** to be invited **8.** to visit **9.** to make **10.** to talk **11.** to tell **12.** (to) imagine **13.** (to) try **14.** to go **15.** to be attacked **16.** to walk **17.** to go **18.** to drive **19.** to let/to have let **20.** to have been **21.** To lose/To have lost **22.** to have had

5.

2. to learn **3.** to work **4.** To do **5.** to get **6.** To be **7.** to show up **8.** to take **9.** to leave **10.** to do **11.** to give **12.** to have gotten **13.** to be given/to have been given **14.** to be taken advantage of/to have been taken advantage of **15.** to invest **16.** to have been tricked **17.** to tell **18.** to forget **19.** to pursue **20.** to be **21.** to talk **22.** to be told **23.** To get **24.** to behave **25.** to go out

6.

to maintaining → to maintain   to expanding → to expand
to illustrates → to illustrate   to knitting → to knit
meeting women → to meet women   for to socialize with
→ to socialize with   invited dine → invited to dine
needed cook → needed to cook   took up to run → took
up running   expects being awarded → expects to be
awarded   interest in to ice skate → interest in ice skating
preparing open → preparing to open   volunteers teach →
volunteers to teach   serve demonstrate → serve to
demonstrate   be encouraged accept → be encouraged to
accept   To having → To have   should not hope attain →
should not hope to attain   enough just work out →
enough just to work out   suddenly be able → suddenly to
be able   to go to downhill ski or tango dance → to go
downhill skiing or tango dancing   expect being able →
expect to be able   can manage live → can manage to live
advised taking life easy → advised to take life easy   avoid
to be alone → avoid being alone

7.

(Answers will vary.)

PART V: Adverbials and Discourse Connectors

 ## UNIT 12 Adverb Clauses

1.

although family members may argue (contrast)   because
every person needs to know that somebody cares for and
about him or her (reason)   if a person feels connected to
another (condition)   When family members have goals and
support each other's goals (time)   if a parent is hoping to
be promoted at work (condition)   If a youngster is trying
to make the basketball team (condition)   When one family
member is having trouble (time)   Even though this person
doesn't have a job (contrast)   because this person doesn't
have a job (reason)   so [secure] that they know their
families will always be there for them (result)   wherever
you look (place)

2.

2. as soon as **3.** Wherever he goes **4.** less expensive than
5. When you want **6.** less than **7.** If she likes **8.** so
fascinating that

3.

2. As soon as **3.** Until **4.** Wherever **5.** even though **6.** if
7. than **8.** while **9.** so

4.

2. Whenever we turn on the television, we are bombarded
with scenes and stories of violence. OR We are bombarded
with scenes and stories of violence whenever we turn on
the television. **3.** When we go out, we know it is possible
that we will become victims of violence. OR We know it is
possible that we will become victims of violence when we
go out. **4.** In spite of the fact that an ever-increasing
amount of money is being spent on crime, crime rates have
not fallen. OR Crime rates have not fallen in spite of the fact
that an ever-increasing amount of money is being spent on
crime. **5.** As long as the public can't agree on how to fight
crime, there is little that can really be done. OR There is
little that can really be done as long as the public can't
agree on how to fight crime. **6.** Because we need to
understand violence better, we are searching for its causes.
7. Since children in strong families tend to become socially
responsible citizens, we need to take steps to strengthen
the family. OR We need to take steps to strengthen the
family since children in strong families tend to become
socially responsible citizens.

5.

While animals on the lower end of the scale they display →
While animals on the lower end of the scale display   If
when we watch → If we watch/When we watch   because
wherever conformity → because conformity   Whether the
sport it is → Whether the sport is   long before became →
long before it became   wherever was there enough
space → wherever there was enough space   sports are of
so interest that → sports are of such interest that
Although young people are especially interested →
Because/Since/On account of the fact that young people are
especially interested   Because that you want → Because
you want

6.

(Answers will vary.)

Adverbials: Viewpoint, Focus, and Negative

1.

Just almost Unfortunately hardly only almost scarcely Not only Never never Obviously Maybe simply Maybe merely Luckily rarely Actually really even clearly just Frankly at all Little even just Only

2.

2. But really he used up the state's money. OR But he really used up the state's money. 3. He put only his cronies in the best jobs. 4. He even paid for their so-called business trips. 5. He did merely the minimal work. 6. He simply appeared in his office, dispensed favors, and went out to play golf. 7. He just didn't care about the people of this state. 8. This state will be saved only if you elect Don Deare.

3.

2. Seldom does he take a vacation. 3. Rarely is he able to spend much time with them. 4. Never does he neglect his family. 5. On no account would he accept a bribe. 6. Only then does he make a decision. 7. Little do people realize how many hours he has volunteered at the shelter for the homeless. 8. Never does he think of himself first. 9. Not only has he served the people very well as a civic volunteer, but he will do even more for them as a senator.

4.

2. We clearly agree that steps must be taken to strengthen the family. 3A. Sadly, there is another factor that must be considered, however—the influence of TV violence. B. There is, sadly, another factor that must be considered, however—the influence of TV violence. 4. We encounter scenes of violence wherever we look, even in cartoon shows and programs for families. 5A. Unfortunately, our children can't help seeing these scenes. B. Our children, unfortunately, can't help seeing these scenes. C. Our children can't help seeing these scenes, unfortunately. 6. Not only must we take action to strengthen the family, but we must pressure our legislators to stop TV violence. 7A. Obviously, much needs to be done. B. Much needs to be done, obviously. C. Much, obviously, needs to be done. 8A. Hopefully, we will win the war against violent programs. B. We will, hopefully, win the war against violent programs. C. We will win the war against violent programs, hopefully. 9A. Fortunately, we can limit our children's TV viewing. B. We can, fortunately, limit our children's TV viewing. C. We can limit our children's TV viewing, fortunately. 10. This means allowing only programs that do not show violence. 11. Other programs are, simply, "off limits." 12. We also have to help our children develop interests so they will not be tempted at all to sit glued to the TV. OR We also have to help our children develop interests so they will not be at all tempted to sit glued to the TV. OR We also have to help our children develop interests so they will not at all be tempted to sit glued to the TV.

5.

battling hard really → really battling hard/battling really hard the only best players → only the best players seldom amateurs appear → seldom do amateurs appear/amateurs seldom appear is to simply score → is simply to score A player hopefully gets → Hopefully, a player gets is as just fierce as → is just as fierce as never gives nothing → never gives anything is won through only a hard fight → is won only through a hard fight not only it is necessary → not only is it necessary To obviously know the words is important → Obviously, to know the words is important/To know the words is important, obviously/To know the words, obviously, is important is more even important → is even more important know how just to place the letters → know just how to place the letters even there is → there is even At all this is not the image → This is not at all the image mathematical wizards play only this game → only mathematical wizards play this game One hundred sixty-seven actually different occupations → Actually, 167 different occupations Little it is known → Little is it known as just vigorously as → just as vigorously as

6.

(Answers will vary.)

Other Discourse Connectors

1.

As a result Moreover In addition therefore However In fact Next but so besides that nevertheless Finally For one thing and along with On the other hand or and Meanwhile

2.

2. but 3. As a result 4. First 5. Second 6. Third 7. for example 8. To sum up 9. in contrast 10. and 11. Also

3.

2. but 3. in fact 4. As a result 5. Furthermore 6. In contrast 7. Moreover 8. so 9. nor

4.

2. Instead 3. First 4. Otherwise 5. In addition 6. And 7. finally 8. so 9. Despite 10. For instance 11. Along with 12. but 13. Besides

5.

The following answers are suggested. In some cases other answers are possible.   however → but   Because → Therefore/Consequently   and → also/in addition   or → nor   however the fact → despite the fact   also → and

nevertheless → but   but → however   Although → However   consequently → because of

6.

(Answers will vary.)

UNIT 15 Adverbial Modifying Phrases

1.

While struggling with the demands presented by a
  population grown too fast
creating more problems than solutions
Having caused such strains that our government can no
  longer effectively serve us
by limiting the number of high-density buildings permitted
  to be built in certain areas
by discouraging outsiders from investing in our city
By taking concrete measures like these
Faced with a tough choice between limiting our population
  and letting our standards of living slip

2.

2. Having been **3.** Having lost **4.** To ensure **5.** not having **6.** stressed **7.** spreading **8.** bringing

3.

2. Having been told . . . /Told that vitamin C, vitamin E, and beta-carotene greatly reduce cancer risk, people began buying these nutrients in large quantities. **3.** Informed that taking one aspirin a day lessens the chances of having a heart attack, people began taking aspirin. **4.** Having learned that one glass of wine per day has a beneficial effect on the heart and circulatory system, many people now drink wine for medicinal reasons. **5.** Hoping to lower their cholesterol levels, people minimize their intake of animal fats.
6. Knowing that roughage in the diet is excellent for digestion, people are consuming more fresh fruit, vegetables, and whole wheat products. **7.** Believing that eating a lot of fish will raise their intelligence level, some people eat a lot of fish. **8.** Having known for a long time that too much salt and sugar is unhealthful, people buy a lot of salt-free and sugar-free products. **9.** Realizing that they can contribute to their own good health, people eat much more knowledgeably than they used to.

4.

Found → Finding   to continued → to continue   After having complete → After having completed   When look → When looking   Having find → Having found   to clicking → by clicking   Having join → Having joined   When require → When required   Have obtained → Having obtained   while have → while having

5.

(Answers will vary.)

PART VI: Adjective Clauses

UNIT 16 Review and Expansion

1.

you make when writing or typing
who began using tempera paint to cover up her typing
  errors
whose ink didn't erase as cleanly as that of manual
  typewriters
who was also an artist
which she called Mistake Out
she had bought for the backyard
which turned her down
which came to be called Liquid Paper
which ended about six months before she sold the
  company
of which $3.5 million was net income
she finally sold her business to Gilette in 1979
of whom she is understandably proud
which appeared on an NBC television show for several
  years in the mid-1960s
where he also directs some charities
whose purpose is to provide leading intellectuals with the
  time, space, and compatible colleagues
that they need to ponder and articulate the most important
  social problems of our era
that there was clearly a need for
which is a fine thing to do

2.

2. which **3.** where **4.** who/that **5.** which/that **6.** whom/that/0 **7.** which/that/0 **8.** that/which/0 **9.** whose **10.** who/that **11.** when **12.** which **13.** which/that **14.** which/that **15.** which/that **16.** which/that/0

3.

2. H A beeper is a battery-operated device whose beeping noise indicates when someone is trying to make a phone connection with you. **3.** E An air bag is a device in a car that/which inflates upon collision to prevent injury. **4.** J A microwave oven is an oven in which people cook food quickly./A microwave oven is an oven that/which/0 people cook food quickly in. **5.** A A fax machine is a machine that/which transmits written material instantly by telephone. **6.** G A computer is an electronic device whose function is to store and process data. **7.** I A CD is a small disc on which music is recorded./A CD is a small disc that/which/0 music is recorded on. **8.** B An answering machine is an electronic device that/which records telephone messages. **9.** D An electronic dictionary is a gadget in which you find words by punching in their letters./An electronic dictionary is a gadget that/which/0 you find words in by punching in their letters. **10.** C A VCR is a machine that/which records TV shows for viewing at a future time.

4.

2. B **3.** A **4.** B **5.** A **6.** B **7.** A **8.** B **9.** A **10.** A **11.** B **12.** B

5.

some of them → some of which   whom is nervous → who is nervous   whom rarely smiles → who rarely smiles   to which everything is serious → to whom everything is serious   who they are → who are   whom often suffered → who often suffered   of that others → of whom others   which is probably not → who is probably not   they were born under it → they were born under   who born → who was born   that born → that was born   that are intuitive → who are intuitive   who they are → who are   whose his brain → whose brain   to improve it → to improve   for people are looking → for people who are looking   which it is → which is

6.

(Answers will vary.)

 # UNIT 17 Adjective Clauses with Quantifiers; Adjectival Modifying Phrases

1.

Adjective Clauses: many of which were filmed in remote parts of the world   one of which was called *A Trip to the Moon* and influenced many subsequent filmmakers   some of which involved chase scenes
Adjective Phrases: learning how to fake prizefights, news events, and foreign settings   made with the aid of the microscope   credited with creating methods   leading toward the development of special-effects movies   shot outdoors   a camera operator and director   showing different actions simultaneously   seen and loved even today   changing the world forever

2.

2. most of which could have been avoided **3.** half of which are longer than 40 days **4.** 71 percent of whom think people in power take advantage of others **5.** 14 percent of whom achieve scores of over 130 on IQ tests **6.** more than half of whom are under 64 years old **7.** all of which yield more nutrients when lightly cooked than when raw **8.** much of which is junk food

3.

2. embodied by Catherine Deneuve as a plantation owner **3.** surrounding her **4.** transformed by a magic spell **5.** reunited for a funeral **6.** raising a lion cub in Kenya **7.** enlisted to impersonate the president of the United States **8.** falling into trouble as they emigrate to America **9.** held in captivity **10.** fighting to save Africa's gorillas from extinction **11.** again separated from his vacationing family   facing similar woes **12.** becoming involved with a wealthy family

4.

2. Then, there are various places where you can buy computers, including computer stores, electronics stores, office supply stores, and mail-order houses. **3.** At reasonable prices, ranging from $1,200 to $3,000, you can get everything you need. **4.** Within this price range, of course, you will find varying capabilities among the computers, many of which come equipped with a fax/modem. **5.** Many major brands of computer have a toll-free number, given to customers so that they may call the company for technical assistance. **6.** If you are a new buyer, having little experience with computers, you should buy from a store where you know you can get help. **7.** While you are shopping around, you will find words like *hard drive, megabyte,* and *CD-ROM drive,* all of which are part of a computer owner's vocabulary. **8.** If you need your computer while you're traveling, you should consider a laptop, small enough and light enough to carry with you. **9.** Sometimes computers come with programs already installed at the factory. **10.** You don't have to buy many extra capabilities, unneeded by beginners, right away. **11.** For newcomers to computers, it's a good idea to take some classes or to get a tutor, both of which can usually be arranged for by the store.

5.

making in 1945 → made in 1945   that produced for entertainment value → produced for entertainment value   showed the harshness of life → showing the harshness of life   was an outstanding director → an outstanding director   the most famous of them is → the most famous of which is   which a movie → a movie   calling the "New Wave" → called the "New Wave"   seeing in movies → seen in movies   was known as the "Angry Young Man" movement → known as the "Angry Young Man" movement

some of them are masterfully explored → some of which are masterfully explored   was the first Asian filmmaker → the first Asian filmmaker   portray the problems of the individual → portraying the problems of the individual   included Shakespeare's plays → including Shakespeare's plays   many of them were focusing → many of which were focusing

6.

(Answers will vary.)

PART VII: Noun Clauses

Noun Clauses: Subjects and Objects

1.

that ruthlessness in modern war is necessary
that sacrificing one's life and the lives of others is glorious
That all a nation's able-bodied men give compulsory military service
whoever was able
What took place in the United States
why people go to war
whether any territorial imperative, commercial advantage, or religious belief can justify the loss of even one life
whatever we can to end conscription everywhere
that no cause, however just, is rationale enough to force a man to fight to kill

2.

2. Who talked to the boss about Charlie **3.** Where Charlie is now **4.** When Charlie is going to be arrested **5.** When the money was stolen **6.** What will happen to Charlie
7. Whether or not Charlie is a thief **8.** we have a big-time embezzler in our company **9.** What I think about this news

3.

2. that a school's curriculum should include a strong sports program **3.** what students can do to become part of a team **4.** whoever is interested in a sport and tries hard **5.** whatever training is necessary **6.** that the training is difficult **7.** what he or she has to do **8.** where he or she belongs **9.** what it feels like to be a team player

4.

how does a person find → how a person finds   concluded that is it → concluded that it is   questioned what were the real values in life → questioned what the real values in life were   whomever opposed → whoever opposed   feel that war it → feel that war   whatever convictions do they personally hold → whatever convictions they personally hold   for that would normally be → for what would normally be   for whatever in the world → for wherever in the world

5.

(Answers will vary.)

Complementation

1.

(that) a direct way of speaking is more effective than an indirect way of speaking and is also a sign of power and self-confidence (adjective complement)
that the degree of directness of speech varies greatly among cultures (subject complement)
that both women and men are indirect (adjective complement)
that directness always works best (adjective complement)
that one of the subordinates will close the window right away (subject complement)

that the subordinate quickly find and present the information (adjective complement)
that more than the choice of vocabulary and tone of voice determine whether a command is successful (adjective complement)
that the status of the speaker and the listener be mutually understood (subject complement)
that both people interact in accordance with the unwritten rules of this understanding (subject complement)

2.

2. that I forget about Lisa 3. that this is much easier said than done 4. that I can't forget about her 5. that I am not receptive to meeting people 6. that I get my life in order 7. that you be responsible on the job 8. that you have always been too casual about your work 9. that you keep the next job you get 10. that you adopt a better attitude 11. that you not invest any more money in bad deals

3.

2. C It is necessary that time be taken to do a job right.
3. F It is advisable that you not criticize others for faults you have. 4. H It is essential that things be done in the right order. 5. B It is advisable that problems be taken care of before they get worse. 6. I It is important that you not be upset over what already happened. 7. G It is desirable that a person stick with what he or she already has rather than going after other things. 8. A It is vital

that a person enjoy life as well as work. 9. D It is essential that a person get an early start to beat the competition. 10. J It is necessary that precautions be taken *before* there is trouble.

4.

The fact it is that students → The fact is that students If it is clear that experiencing Mozart raise → If it is clear that experiencing Mozart raises in the background it seems clear → in the background seems clear obvious to the parents because that → obvious to the parents that insist that the child listens → insist that the child listen insist that something is done → insist that something be done problem is it that → problem is that

5.

(Answers will vary.)

PART VIII: Unreal Conditions

UNIT 20 Unreal Conditionals and Other Ways to Express Unreality

1.

If he hadn't, the delicious substance might never have crossed the ocean to Spain.

If it hadn't been so expensive, the masses could have enjoyed it much sooner.

If this chocolatier hadn't, we would not have the wide range of candies and candy bars that we have today.

If he hadn't, Switzerland and the Netherlands would not have become the great producers of quality chocolates that they are.

if he hadn't, we would not have chocolate cakes or chocolate chip cookies.

if there were not such a well-developed world trade, chocolate lovers would not be ale to indulge themselves so easily.

if their fat and sugar intake were lower, they would be healthier.

". . . if I had a day without chocolate, it would be like a day without sunshine."

2.

2. was brought back to Europe by the Spanish explorers is popular today 3. are not healthy eat a lot of chocolate and other foods containing fat and sugar 4. don't eat a balanced diet are not well nourished 5. have enough will-power to refuse junk food 6. consumed 4,000 calories at the last meal that they ate 7. is a tomorrow 8. isn't easy

3.

2. I met the right man, I would have a different feeling about it 3. I didn't have a lot of friends, I would be lonely 4. I didn't like my job, I would be unhappy 5. (that) people would leave me alone 6. I were a weird person 7. I could meet the perfect man tomorrow 8. (that) I had it all/I could have it all 9. (that) I meet somebody 10. that's an excellent matchmaking service 11. they introduce me to someone perfect

4.

2. would never have met 3. would have failed 4. hadn't wasted 5. wouldn't have had to eat 6. would have known 7. wouldn't have been 8. wouldn't have suffered 9. had met 10. hadn't fallen asleep 11. wouldn't have been able to 12. had never met 13. hadn't happened 14. hadn't made 15. would have passed

5.

would called her up → would call her up would never had met → would never have met wish we have already been → wish we had already been as though I knew her → as though I'd known her/as though I've known her would liked her → would like her what did she say → what would she say as though we are kids → as though we were kids hope that you answered → hope that you answer

6.

(Answers will vary.)

Inverted and Implied Conditionals; Subjunctive in Noun Clauses

1.

Without (the simple little tool that we take for granted)
(essential that we) have
What if (we had no way of preserving . . .)
Without (canned tuna)
if not (used correctly)
Had the U.S. military not adopted this primitive can opener in the Civil War . . .
otherwise (we would not have the convenience . . .)

2.

2. that he or she drive on the left **3.** that people remove their shoes before going inside a house **4.** that people keep their shoes on **5.** that people not eat pork products **6.** that pork products be avoided **7.** that a sick person take vitamin C **8.** that a sick person have a lot of homemade chicken soup **9.** that a waiter be summoned by whistling **10.** that a waiter not be summoned by whistling **11.** that a traveler learn about customs in various places

3.

2. not gained, would have remained **3.** might not have won **4.** would not have grown **5.** rejected, would not have become **6.** not won, would have gained **7.** would have died **8.** lived, would have served

4.

2. we would have to use our fingers to eat **3.** not been discovered, we wouldn't have electric lights, movies, television, or computers **4.** existed in the last century, people would have traveled extensively then **5.** not available throughout the world, fashion, music, and basic values would not be very similar in many places **6.** not been developed, businesses wouldn't be able to obtain the data they need to function in today's competitive world. **7.** the general public wouldn't have easy access to extensive knowledge

5.

plants would stayed healthy → plants would stay healthy
we will be free → we would be free   people could lived longer → people could live longer   If had scientists already discovered → Had scientists already discovered/If scientists had already discovered   there will be no crime → there would be no crime   we don't have the United Nations → we wouldn't have the United Nations
we will not have found the means → we would not have found the means   we did not have cleaned up → we would not have cleaned up   that the *haves* . . . made concrete contributions → that the *haves* . . . make concrete contributions   that citizens gave a specified amount → that citizens give a specified amount   that hope is expressed → that hope be expressed

6.

(Answers will vary.)

TEST: UNITS 1–3

PART ONE

DIRECTIONS: Circle the letter of the correct answer to complete each sentence.

Example:

Dolphins, _____ porpoises, are well known for   **A**   **B**   Ⓒ   **D**

their ability to delight humans with their antics.

  A. alike

  B. that they are like

  C. like

  D. which are alike

1. Construction of the Brooklyn Bridge, the first steel-wire   **A**   **B**   **C**   **D**

    suspension bridge in the world, _____

    in 1869 but wasn't finished until 1893.

  A. was beginning

  B. has begun

  C. began

  D. beginning

2. The American skater was not as good as many of the   **A**   **B**   **C**   **D**

    other skaters. She _____ possibly have

    won the gold medal.

  A. couldn't

  B. could

  C. must

  D. might

3. By the time the monorail is completed next year, the taxpayers   **A**   **B**   **C**   **D**

_____ over $22 million for a transportation

system already obsolete.

A. will spend

B. will be spending

C. will have spent

D. will have been spending

4. Since the use of antibiotics _____ widespread,   **A**   **B**   **C**   **D**

certain types of pneumonia and streptococcal infections

are no longer as terrifying as they once were.

A. was becoming

B. has become

C. had become

D. become

5. By the time the ancient Egyptian civilization began to flourish   **A**   **B**   **C**   **D**

more than 5,000 years ago, the onion _____

a staple food throughout the Middle East for many years.

A. had already been

B. was already

C. has already been

D. would have been

6. Before the construction of the Panama Canal, ships   **A**   **B**   **C**   **D**

_____ around the tip of South America to

get to the Pacific Ocean from the Atlantic.

A. should have traveled

B. must have traveled

C. had to travel

D. have traveled

7. Because the river _____ steadily since

Sunday, the residents of the area have been advised to

prepare for flood conditions.

A. rose

B. had risen

C. is rising

D. has been rising

A   B   C   D

8. John F. Kennedy, not expected to win the American

presidential election of 1960, in fact _____

by a small majority.

A. has won

B. had to win

C. did win

D. should have won

A   B   C   D

9. The best diamonds are transparent and colorless, but diamonds

actually _____ in color from clear to black.

A. range

B. are ranging

C. ranged

D. have been ranging

A   B   C   D

10. Years before the Empress Masako assumed her role in Japan,

she _____ at Harvard University.

A. would study

B. used to study

C. was used to study

D. used to studying

A   B   C   D

PART TWO

DIRECTIONS: Each sentence has four underlined words or phrases. The four underlined parts of the sentence are marked A, B, C, and D. Circle the letter of the <u>one</u> underlined word or phrase that is NOT CORRECT.

Example:

Peope in <u>every part</u> of the world now <u>readily</u> and easily
            A   B

<u>communicates</u> <u>by means</u> of electronic mail.
    C   D

A   **B**   Ⓒ   **D**

11. The notion that a cat <u>can fall</u> from a great height and <u>survived</u>
                     A   B

    is true and <u>may have contributed</u> to the idea that a cat <u>has</u>
                     C   D

    nine lives.

A   **B**   **C**   **D**

12. Because the beaches <u>are eroding</u> at an alarming rate for the
                     A

    past ten years, the state government <u>no longer</u> <u>permits</u>
                                      B   C

    <u>building</u> within 100 yards of the coastal area.
    D

A   **B**   **C**   **D**

13. The Rosetta Stone, a basalt slab <u>inscribed</u> by priests more than
                                      A

    2,000 years ago, <u>has been</u> discovered by Napoleon's troops in
                     B

    1799 and <u>has provided</u> scholars with the key to <u>translating</u>
                C   D

    Egyptian hieroglyphics.

A   **B**   **C**   **D**

14. Social scientists <u>wonder</u> just how many of today's children
                  A

    <u>will be reading</u> regularly in twenty years after they <u>would watch</u>
    B   C

    television for more than a thousand hours per year <u>during</u>
                                          D

    their childhood.

A   **B**   **C**   **D**

15. Archaeologists <u>believe</u> that the Mayan Indian civilization <u>may have</u>
                A   B

    <u>been originating</u> around 1000 B.C. in north-central Guatemala, where

    evidence of a once-flourishing agricultural people <u>has</u> <u>been found</u>.
                                              C   D

A   **B**   **C**   **D**

16. <u>Using</u> carbolic acid as an antiseptic agent in conjunction with
   A

<u>sterilizing</u> instruments, Joseph Lister <u>was introducing</u> the principle
   B   C

of antiseptics to surgery in 1865 and dramatically <u>reduced</u> the
                                        D

number of postoperative fatalities.

    A   **B**   **C**   **D**

17. The English words *diamond* and *adamant* both <u>are coming</u> from
                                        A

the Greek word *adamas,* which <u>means</u> invincible and at first
                         B

<u>referred</u> to all hard metals and then to the diamond <u>exclusively</u>.
  C   D

    A   **B**   **C**   **D**

18. Linguists <u>have observed</u> that when men and women <u>are talking</u>,
          A   B

men <u>interrupt</u> the conversations much more frequently and
      C

generally <u>have listened</u> less.
            D

    A   **B**   **C**   **D**

19. Some observers <u>think</u> that if we don't <u>reduce</u> our consumption, by
               A   B

the middle of the next century, our resources <u>might be insufficient</u>
                                                C

and many people <u>must be hungry</u>.
                  D

    A   **B**   **C**   **D**

20. Until the Chunnel <u>was actually built</u>, it <u>was widely believed</u> that
                      A   B

<u>traveling</u> between France and England by train <u>will never be</u> possible.
  C   D

    A   **B**   **C**   **D**

TEST: UNITS 4–7

PART ONE

DIRECTIONS: Circle the letter of the correct answer to complete each sentence.

Example:

Dolphins, _____ porpoises, are well known for   A   B   Ⓒ   D

their ability to delight humans with their antics.

   A. alike

   B. that they are like

   C. like

   D. which are alike

1. Because of the emphasis on nutrition in recent decades,   A   B   C   D

   Americans now consume _____ poultry and

   fish and much less beef.

   A. a number of

   B. a great deal of

   C. either

   D. many

2. On much of television today, _____ presented   A   B   C   D

   more frequently than straightforward information.

   A. a sensational news is

   B. sensational news is

   C. sensational news are

   D. some sensational news are

3. There are few, if any, _____ more important
than honesty in the assessment of a person's character.

    A   B   C   D

A. criterion that is

B. criteria that are

C. criterias that is

D. criterions that are

4. _____ certain molds and fungi to multiply
very rapidly.

    A   B   C   D

A. A tropical weather causes

B. Tropical weather cause

C. The tropical weather cause

D. Tropical weather causes

5. After the flood, many schools remained closed for several days
because of the concern about _____.

    A   B   C   D

A. a health

B. some health

C. children health

D. health

6. A common stereotype existing until the mid-twentieth century
held that _____ usually happy and jolly.

    A   B   C   D

A. fat people is

B. a fat people is

C. fat people are

D. fat peoples are

7. Augusta Ada Byron was _____ who created a   **A**   **B**   **C**   **D**

    program for a theoretical computer in the mid-nineteenth century.

A. an English visionary woman mathematician

B. a visionary English woman mathematician

C. an English woman visionary mathematician

D. a visionary English mathematician woman

8. The Great Depression of 1929 caused the loss of millions of   **A**   **B**   **C**   **D**

    _____ almost impossible to find.

A. the jobs, and the work was

B. job, and work was

C. jobs, and work was

D. jobs, and works were

9. Although occasionally a third party has exhibited some political   **A**   **B**   **C**   **D**

    strength, the United States has essentially _____

    political system.

A. two parties

B. a two-parties

C. the two parties'

D. a two-party

10. Not _____ from South Africa, although most   **A**   **B**   **C**   **D**

    of the world's supply does originate there.

A. every gold comes

B. all gold come

C. all gold comes

D. every gold come

PART TWO

DIRECTIONS: Each sentence has four underlined words or phrases. The four underlined parts of the sentence are marked A, B, C, and D. Circle the letter of the <u>one</u> underlined word or phrase that is NOT CORRECT.

Example:

People in <u>every part</u> of the world now <u>readily</u> and easily   **A**   **B**   Ⓒ   **D**
             A   B
<u>communicates</u> <u>by means</u> of electronic mail.
    C   D

11. <u>Horses races</u> are recorded <u>as early as</u> 1500 B.C. in Egypt, but
       A   B

     <u>the organized sport</u> dates <u>from twelfth-century England</u>.
          C   D

12. <u>Well adapted</u> to their <u>long, cold winters</u>, Eskimos have   **A**   **B**   **C**   **D**
       A   B

     traditionally obtained <u>each of their</u> food, clothing, oil, tools, and
                      C

     weapons from <u>sea mammals</u>.
              D

13. <u>Hypnosis</u>, the term for <u>a psychological state</u> that superficially   **A**   **B**   **C**   **D**
      A   B

     resembles <u>sleep</u>, is generally induced by the monotonous repetition
              C

     <u>of word</u> and gestures while the subject is completely relaxed.
      D

14. <u>Much of</u> a person's character, psychologists believe, is formed by   **A**   **B**   **C**   **D**
      A

     the environmental <u>influences</u> of <u>the five first</u> years <u>of life</u>.
                   B   C   D

15. <u>Travelers</u> are usually discouraged by <u>a medical</u> advice from   **A**   **B**   **C**   **D**
      A   B

     visiting <u>those areas</u> where <u>cholera and malaria</u> are epidemic.
            C   D

16. The study of <u>matter</u> and energy in the universe, <u>astronomy</u> is   **A**   **B**   **C**   **D**
              A   B

     probably <u>oldest of</u> the pure <u>sciences</u>.
           C   D

17. <u>In the</u> 1920s and 1930s, <u>new</u> furniture style called Art Deco,   **A**   **B**   **C**   **D**
     A   B

     which featured more comfortable and informal <u>furniture</u> than had
                                      C

     been <u>in style</u> previously, became internationally fashionable.
          D

18. <u>Played</u> <u>in few parts</u> of the world outside of the United States,
     A   B

     <u>the baseball</u> <u>first</u> became an event in the Olympic Games in 1984.
        C   D

         A   B   C   D

19. The largest country <u>in area</u> in <u>the Western</u> Hemisphere, Brazil is
                 A   B

     <u>only country</u> in the hemisphere <u>where Portuguese</u> is the first
        C   D

     language.

         A   B   C   D

20. <u>One glass of</u> an ordinary cola drink, containing more caffeine than
        A

     two average cups <u>of coffees,</u> is sufficient to <u>cause agitation</u> in
               B   C

     <u>some young children</u>.
         D

         A   B   C   D

TEST: UNITS 8–9

PART ONE

DIRECTIONS: Circle the letter of the correct answer to complete each sentence.

Example:

Dolphins, _____ porpoises, are well known for   A   B   Ⓒ   D

their ability to delight humans with their antics.

   A. alike

   B. that they are like

   C. like

   D. which are alike

1. In the cultivation of bonsai trees, the plants _____   A   B   C   D

   small and in true proportion to their natural models by growing

   them in small containers.

A. keep

B. are keeping

C. are kept

D. kept

2. When tornadoes _____ over water, they are called   A   B   C   D

   waterspouts.

A. occur

B. are occurred

C. have occurred

D. have been occurred

3. The Great Wall of China was the only man-made structure on   **A**   **B**   **C**   **D**

earth which _____ when they were circling

the earth.

A. could see by the astronauts

B. could be seen by the astronauts

C. the astronauts could be seen

D. could see the astronauts

4. In spite of the severity of the crash, no one _____,   **A**   **B**   **C**   **D**

which is attributed to the fact all four passengers were wearing

their safety belts.

A. was even slightly injuring

B. that they were slightly injured

C. even slightly injured

D. was even slightly injured

5. The characters of the novelist Isaac Bashevis Singer frequently   **A**   **B**   **C**   **D**

suffer loneliness and alienation and _____.

A. often tormented by demons

B. demons are often tormented them

C. are often tormented by demons

D. often have tormented by demons

6. The western genre of film, like the gangster film,   **A**   **B**   **C**   **D**

_____ on depicting simple moral conflicts

between good and evil.

A. found

B. was founded

C. has found

D. founded

7. In a most spectacular manifestation of computer crime, the   A   B   C   D

defendant _____ to have stolen $47 million

from banks and securities firms.

A. is alleged

B. alleges

C. has alleged

D. being alleged

8. Cloisonne, a method of decorating metal surfaces with enamel,   A   B   C   D

_____ in the Middle East and perfected by the

Chinese, Japanese, and French.

A. probably invented

B. was probably invented

C. had probably invented

D. must have invented

9. Almost all automobiles driven in the United States   A   B   C   D

_____ until after World War II, when many

foreign-made cars began to be popular.

A. made in Detroit

B. had been made in Detroit

C. were made in Detroit

D. being made in Detroit

10. Rasputin _____ responsible for many of the   A   B   C   D

ill-fated events that occurred during the reign of Czar Nicholas II

of Russia.

A. believed to be

B. was believed to have been

C. they believed him to be

D. was believing to be

PART TWO

*DIRECTIONS: Each sentence has four underlined words or phrases. The four
underlined parts of the sentence are marked A, B, C, and D. Circle the letter of
the <u>one</u> underlined word or phrase that is NOT CORRECT.*

Example:

People in <u>every part</u> of the world now <u>readily</u> and easily
       A   B
<u>communicates</u> <u>by means</u> of electronic mail.
   C   D

A   B   Ⓒ   D

11. In northern <u>climates</u>, <u>it considered</u> of prime importance to get
             A   B
    the <u>crops harvested</u> by mid-October, before the heavy winter
          C
    <u>snowstorms arrive</u>.
        D

A   B   C   D

12. The modern horse <u>evolved</u> in North America, <u>spread</u> all over
               A   B
    the world, and <u>hunted</u> by early man and <u>domesticated</u> by Asian
              C   D
    nomads as early as the 3rd millennium B.C.

A   B   C   D

13. Singapore <u>was a sparsely populated island</u> when it was <u>purchased</u>
                   A   B
    <u>the East India Company</u> in 1819 through the efforts of Sir
    T. S. Raffles, <u>after whom</u> the capital's most famous hotel <u>is named</u>.
                 C   D

A   B   C   D

14. <u>Resembling</u> the giraffe, to which <u>it is related</u>, the okapi <u>is find</u> in
    A   B   C
    the rain forests of the upper Congo River and <u>was unknown</u> to
                                    D
    zoologists until the early twentieth century.

A   B   C   D

15. In Shakespeare's famous drama, which <u>is known</u> to be <u>based</u> on
                              A   B
    fact, Macbeth seizes the Scottish throne by killing Duncan in
    battle and <u>is then defeated</u> and <u>kill</u> by Duncan's son.
              C   D

A   B   C   D

16. It <u>has long been suspected</u> that <u>consuming</u> large quantities of fish
       A   B
    <u>raises</u> the level of intelligence, but this theory has <u>never proved</u>.
     C   D

A   B   C   D

17. It could never <u>have predicted</u> that the group of four <u>young British</u>
　　　　　　　　　　A　　　　　　　　　　　　　　　　　　　　　　　　　B

rock musicians <u>would attain</u> such popularity after they
　　　　　　　　　　C

<u>had been seen</u> only once on American television.
　　　D

　　　　　　　　　　　　　　　　　　　　　　　　　　　　　A　　B　　C　　D

18. Before photography <u>was invented</u>, people of means <u>had</u> their
　　　　　　　　　　　　　　　　A　　　　　　　　　　　　　　　B

pictures <u>painting</u> by famous artists so that their images <u>would</u>
　　　　　　C　　　　　　　　　　　　　　　　　　　　　　　　　　D

<u>be remembered</u> forever.

　　　　　　　　　　　　　　　　　　　　　　　　　　　　　A　　B　　C　　D

19. Famous as a <u>silver-tongued</u> orator, William Jennings Bryan never
　　　　　　　　　　　A

<u>had to be shouted</u> to make <u>himself heard</u> by the adoring crowds
　　　B　　　　　　　　　　　　　　C

<u>that were spellbound</u> by his every word.
　　　D

　　　　　　　　　　　　　　　　　　　　　　　　　　　　　A　　B　　C　　D

20. The police <u>are still mystified</u> by the lack of clues regarding the
　　　　　　　A

kidnapping, which <u>must have committed</u>　<u>by a person</u>　<u>who was</u>
　　　　　　　　　　B　　　　　　　　　　　　C　　　　　　　D

<u>known</u> to the victims.

　　　　　　　　　　　　　　　　　　　　　　　　　　　　　A　　B　　C　　D

TEST: UNITS 10–11

PART ONE

DIRECTIONS: Circle the letter of the correct answer to complete each sentence.

Example:

Dolphins, _____ porpoises, are well known for   A   B   Ⓒ   D

their ability to delight humans with their antics.

   A. alike

   B. that they are like

   C. like

   D. which are alike

1. The environmental group hopes _____ the   A   B   C   D

    forest to its original condition by the end of the decade.

A. having restored

B. to have restored

C. to be restored

D. to have been restored

2. It is almost axiomatic that middle-aged people regret   A   B   C   D

    _____ some of the excesses of their youth.

A. to have been commited

B. the committing

C. to commit

D. having committed

3. Many of the early British settlers in Australia were convicts who   A   B   C   D

were able to avoid _____ by agreeing to live

on and develop the land there.

A. be imprisoned

B. to be imprisoned

C. being imprisoned

D. imprisoned

4. Because of an abnormally high accident rate, restrictions on   A   B   C   D

teenagers' _____ are being considered.

A. drive

B. having driving

C. driving

D. to drive

5. The Japanese art of origami is based on _____   A   B   C   D

paper into various forms.

A. fold

B. to fold

C. to have folded

D. folding

6. Believed _____ from Polynesia in canoes in   A   B   C   D

early times, the Maori established an agricultural society in

New Zealand.

A. to migrate

B. to have migrated

C. migrating

D. having migrated

7. Surprisingly, the largest clubs in North America for

    _____ are found in the southern cities of

    Atlanta and Miami.

A. to ski

B. ski

C. skiing

D. to skiing

A   B   C   D

8. Diners who had been exposed to the hepatitis virus in the

    restaurant were advised _____ a gamma

    globulin injection.

A. to get

B. to have gotten

C. getting

D. having gotten

A   B   C   D

9. More than 2,300 people in the state volunteered

    _____ clean up the mess that the oil spill

    had created on the shore.

A. to have helped

B. having helped

C. to help

D. helping

A   B   C   D

10. The Oscar winner so appreciated _____ to

    receive the highest honor of her profession that she nearly

    cried during her acceptance speech.

A. to choose

B. choosing

C. having been chosen

D. to have been chosen

A   B   C   D

PART TWO

DIRECTIONS: Each sentence has four underlined words or phrases. The four underlined parts of the sentence are marked A, B, C, and D. Circle the letter of the <u>one</u> underlined word or phrase that is NOT CORRECT.

Example:

People in <u>every part</u> of the world now <u>readily</u> and easily   A   B   Ⓒ   D
<u>communicates</u> <u>by means</u> of electronic mail.
　　A　　　　　　　　　B
　　　C　　　　　D

11. Toy manufacturers must be extremely careful <u>to making</u> their   A   B   C   D
　　products safe in order <u>to protect</u> the children <u>who use</u> them
　　　　　　　　　　　A
　　from <u>being injured</u>.
　　　　　　B　　　　　　　　　C
　　　　　D

12. An American literary legend, Tom Sawyer was able <u>to get</u> his   A   B   C   D
　　friends <u>paint</u> the fence <u>by</u> <u>pretending</u> that the chore was a
　　　　　　　　　　　　A
　　special privilege.
　　　　B　　　　　　C　　　D

13. Doctors sometimes <u>use hypnosis</u> on patients who have been   A   B   C   D
　　trying <u>to stop</u> <u>to smoke</u> without <u>succeeding</u>.
　　　　　　　　　A
　　　　　B　　　C　　　　　　D

14. In 1938, Anna Freud <u>was forced</u> <u>emigrating</u> from Vienna to   A   B   C   D
　　England, where she managed <u>to found</u> and <u>direct</u> a successful
　　　　　　　　A　　　B
　　clinic for child therapy.
　　　　　　　　　C　　　　D

15. <u>In order to</u> <u>be consider</u> <u>for admission to</u> some top universities, a   A   B   C   D
　　candidate needs <u>to have scored</u> more than 600 on the TOEFL test.
　　　A　　　　B　　　　　C
　　　　　　　　D

16. <u>The moment</u> that the plane touched down safely, the passengers   A   B   C   D
　　expressed their gratitude for <u>having survived</u> the <u>harrowing flight</u>
　　　A
　　by <u>having been applauded</u> the pilot and crew.
　　　　　　B　　　　　　　　C
　　　　D

17. <u>Believing</u> it <u>to promote</u> strength and courage, the ancient Roman   A   B   C   D
　　soldiers liked to <u>ate</u> garlic before <u>engaging</u> in battle.
　　　A　　　B
　　　　　　　C　　　　　　D

18. To <u>makeing</u> a perfect score of 300 in a bowling match is an   **A**   **B**   **C**   **D**
     A

accomplishment bowlers rarely attain, although <u>exciting</u>
                                           B

competition results from <u>their</u> trying <u>to</u>.
                          C   D

19. The French impressionist painters <u>attempted</u> <u>to depict</u> transitory   **A**   **B**   **C**   **D**
                                      A   B

visual impressions and <u>achieving</u> brilliance and luminosity by
                                 C

<u>using</u> broken color.
  D

20. Even <u>being considering</u> <u>for nomination</u> to the advisory committee   **A**   **B**   **C**   **D**
                  A   B

is an honor <u>not to be taken</u> lightly or <u>ignored</u>.
               C   D

TEST: UNITS 12–15

PART ONE

DIRECTIONS: Circle the letter of the correct answer to complete each sentence.

Example:

Dolphins, _____ porpoises, are well known for   A   B   Ⓒ   D

their ability to delight humans with their antics.

   A. alike

   B. that they are like

   C. like

   D. which are alike

1. Never before in the history of the country _____   A   B   C   D

   as spiritually united as they were during the war.

   A. the people were

   B. the people had been

   C. had the people been

   D. when the people were

2. The Industrial Revolution created a great need for labor in   A   B   C   D

   factories in cities; _____ the population became

   increasingly less rural and more urban.

   A. so that

   B. consequently,

   C. nevertheless,

   D. otherwise,

3. The Twenty-second Amendment to the Constitution of the United   **A**   **B**   **C**   **D**

States provides for a limitation of the president's time of service,

stating that _____ two terms in office.

A. only the president is limited to

B. the president is limited to only

C. the president is only limited to

D. the president only is limited to

4. Although most citizens desire extensive services from their   **A**   **B**   **C**   **D**

government, _____ is willing to pay higher taxes.

A. but nobody

B. nobody

C. however, nobody

D. so nobody

5. During solar eclipses, people are advised to view the sun directly   **A**   **B**   **C**   **D**

only while _____ through a very small hole in a

piece of cardboard.

A. they have been looking

B. looked

C. looking

D. having looked

6. In the last senatorial election, _____ voted for   **A**   **B**   **C**   **D**

the current senator.

A. 60 percent of the population almost

B. almost 60 percent of the population

C. 60 percent of the population hardly

D. not only 60 percent of the population

7. _____ expenses are so much higher in certain   **A**   **B**   **C**   **D**

cities than in others, companies must provide higher salaries to

its employees in those places.

A. Since

B. Although

C. Because of

D. Only

8. It is projected that by the year 2010, there will be   **A**   **B**   **C**   **D**

_____ people over the age of 65 that the

monies from Social Security won't be sufficient to support them.

A. such

B. so

C. too many

D. so many

9. Wherever overbuilding has taken place along the coast of the   **A**   **B**   **C**   **D**

barrier islands, _____ erosion is occurring.

A. so beach

B. consequently beach

C. beach

D. so that beach

10. Learning to play a musical instrument often motivates a child to   **A**   **B**   **C**   **D**

be disciplined and effective; _____ it can

impart a feeling of social worth.

A. but

B. because

C. so

D. moreover,

PART TWO

DIRECTIONS: Each sentence has four underlined words or phrases. The four underlined parts of the sentence are marked A, B, C, and D. Circle the letter of the <u>one</u> underlined word or phrase that is NOT CORRECT.

Example:

People in <u>every part</u> of the world now <u>readily</u> and easily   A   B   Ⓒ   D
         A
<u>communicates</u> <u>by means</u> of electronic mail.
   C   D

11. <u>Little</u> <u>Columbus did</u> know, <u>crossing</u> the Atlantic in 1492, that his   A   B   C   D
    A   B   C
    voyage <u>would</u> change the course of history forever.
         D

12. Halley's Comet appears <u>so rarely</u> that <u>only do a few</u> people <u>have</u>   A   B   C   D
                      A   B   C
    the opportunity to view it more <u>than once</u> in a lifetime.
                         D

13. <u>Few children</u>, <u>fortunately</u>, get diseases like polio, scarlet fever,   A   B   C   D
     A   B
    and whooping cough <u>anymore</u>, <u>because of</u> immunization
                    C   D
    programs are widespread.

14. <u>Cellular telephones</u> are now <u>such convenient</u> that a business   A   B   C   D
            A   B
    person can and <u>often does save</u> valuable office time by efficiently
                  C
    making telephone calls <u>while driving</u>.
                    D

15. <u>Not only</u> <u>the supply of mahogany has</u> dwindled markedly in the   A   B   C   D
     A   B
    past ten years, but <u>its price has</u> tripled during the same period
                 C
    <u>of time</u>.
     D

16. <u>Having begun</u> his career <u>as a journalist</u>, Federico Fellini   A   B   C   D
        A   B
    became a renowned film director and <u>writer, and</u> winning several
                                 C
    prestigious awards for his <u>works</u>.
                    D

17. <u>When was first setting foot</u> on the moon, Neil Armstrong spoke to   A   B   C   D
             A
    the entire world <u>by</u> television satellite and said that <u>the event</u> was
                  B   C
    a giant leap for <u>mankind</u>.
                 D

18. <u>Having retiring</u> from playing professional tennis, Chris Evert is
      A

now seen <u>commenting</u> on tennis matches <u>and</u> <u>also</u> advertising
            B   C   D

certain products.

                                            A   B   C   D

19. <u>Because</u> Finland is part of Scandinavia, <u>its</u> language is, <u>in fact</u>,
     A   B   C

not like those of the other Scandinavian countries <u>at all</u>.
                                                    D

                                            A   B   C   D

20. <u>Reflected</u> economic conditions as well as social attitudes, the
     A

immigration laws continue <u>to change</u> in order <u>to admit</u> certain
                              B   C

people and <u>refuse entry</u> to others.
                    D

                                            A   B   C   D

TEST: UNITS 16–17

PART ONE

DIRECTIONS: Circle the letter of the correct answer to complete each sentence.

Example:

Dolphins, _____ porpoises, are well known for
their ability to delight humans with their antics.

A   B   Ⓒ   D

   A. alike

   B. that they are like

   C. like

   D. which are alike

1. Tulips, _____ into Holland in 1554, were
quickly and highly valued and soon became the object of wild
financial speculation in Europe.

A   B   C   D

A. which introduced

B. that they were introduced

C. which introduced them

D. introduced

2. Concepts of modern nursing were founded by Florence
Nightingale, an English nurse _____ to the care
of the sick and the war-wounded.

A   B   C   D

A. that she dedicated her life

B. whose life she dedicated

C. whose life was dedicated

D. whose life she dedicated it

3. Relics _____ accidentally while constructing

    a new subway line in Mexico City yielded new information about

    previous civilizations in the area.

A. that workers found them

B. which workers they found

C. that they were found by workers

D. that workers found

    A   B   C   D

4. The advanced course in astrophysics will be open only to those

    graduate students _____ a grade point average

    of 3.8 or above.

A. have

B. they will have

C. having

D. whom have

    A   B   C   D

5. Cork, the second largest city in Ireland, is the site of many

    industries, _____ automobile manufacturing

    and whiskey distilling.

A. some of them are

B. which some are

C. some of which are

D. of which are some

    A   B   C   D

6. Ships traveling in the North Atlantic during the winter must be

    constantly vigilant to avoid icebergs, large masses of ice

    _____ only one-ninth is visible above water.

A. that

B. of that

C. which

D. of which

    A   B   C   D

7. The Olympic Games, _____ in 776 B.C., did not   **A**   **B**   **C**   **D**

include women participants until 1912.

A. they were first played

B. that they were first played

C. which first played

D. first played

8. One of the great fiction writers in English, Charles Dickens wrote   **A**   **B**   **C**   **D**

about all kinds of societal abuses, _____ child

labor, debt imprisonment, and legal injustices.

A. which are including

B. that they include

C. included

D. including

9. *The Mikado,* a warm-hearted spoof of a country   **A**   **B**   **C**   **D**

_____, is one of the best loved works of the

English operetta composers Gilbert and Sullivan.

A. which they knew nothing about

B. that they knew nothing about it

C. about that they knew nothing

D. they know nothing about it

10. Few visitors to Disney World are aware that much of its electrical   **A**   **B**   **C**   **D**

power comes from the energy _____ by burning

its own garbage.

A. that produces

B. producing

C. which it is produced

D. it produces

PART TWO

DIRECTIONS: Each sentence has four underlined words or phrases. The four underlined parts of the sentence are marked A, B, C, and D. Circle the letter of the <u>one</u> underlined word or phrase that is NOT CORRECT.

Example:

People in <u>every part</u> of the world now <u>readily</u> and easily   A   B   Ⓒ   D
<u>communicates</u> <u>by means</u> of electronic mail.
   C   D

11. A famous Danish writer <u>who wrote</u> mainly in English, Isak   A   B   C   D
                 A

    Dinesen is <u>best known</u> <u>for</u> her imaginative tales <u>which containing</u>
             B   C   D

    romantic and supernatural elements.

12. Sunlight sometimes filters through rain droplets in a way <u>that forms</u>   A   B   C   D
                                    A

    a rainbow, <u>which it is</u> an <u>arc composed</u> of every color in the
            B   C

    spectrum and often <u>is regarded</u> as an omen of good luck.
                   D

13. Japanese, <u>which spoken</u> by more than 100 million people,   A   B   C   D
             A

    <u>most of whom live</u> in Japan, appears to be unrelated to <u>any other</u>
         B   C

    language <u>spoken</u> in Asia.
             D

14. Genius is a term <u>which</u> may be used to describe a person <u>whom has</u>   A   B   C   D
               A   B

    a high intelligence or <u>possesses</u> a special aptitude for
                   C

    <u>excelling</u> in a particular field.
      D

15. In a medical study of nearly 5,000 adults, <u>half of who</u> were given   A   B   C   D
                             A

    one aspirin a day while the other half were <u>given</u> a placebo, it was
                               B

    found that <u>those who</u> were taking the aspirin suffered 38 percent
             C

    fewer heart attacks than those <u>who weren't</u>.
                  D

16. A <u>fact not</u> widely known is <u>that</u> Theodore Roosevelt, <u>that was</u> a   A   B   C   D
       A   B   C

    robust and boisterous outdoorsman, had been a weak and sickly

    child <u>who suffered</u> from asthma.
          D

17. Educated women in the last decades of the twentieth century have

been marrying later, <u>which</u> <u>that means</u> <u>that they</u> have fewer
                A   B   C

years <u>in which</u> to produce offspring.
      D

                                                  A   **B**   **C**   **D**

18. Among the stalwart Indians <u>who defeated</u> General George Custer
                                  A

in 1876 was Crazy Horse, a Sioux <u>who</u>, <u>resisted</u> encroachment of
                                  B   C

his lands, <u>had repeatedly defeated</u> U.S. troops in previous battles.
                D

                                                  A   **B**   **C**   **D**

19. Lagos, the capital and largest city of Nigeria, <u>which</u> is comprised
                                            A

<u>of</u> four islands and four inland sections, <u>all of which</u> <u>are connected</u>
 B   C   D

by bridges.

                                                  A   **B**   **C**   **D**

20. Many older couples, <u>whose</u> children have grown and left home,
                         A

move to retirement villages, <u>in where</u> they can participate in
                                B

<u>activities they</u> enjoy and meet people <u>with whom</u> they have
      C   D

much in common.

TEST: UNITS 18–19

PART ONE

DIRECTIONS: Circle the letter of the correct answer to complete each sentence.

Example:

Dolphins, _____ porpoises, are well known for
their ability to delight humans with their antics.

A. alike

B. that they are like

C. like

D. which are alike

A   B   Ⓒ   D

1. In order to avert disaster, it is essential _____
   of the dangers of avalanches in the area.

A. that travelers be advised

B. that travelers they are advised

C. advising travelers

D. where to advise travelers

A   B   C   D

2. _____ the young woman chose to marry didn't
   matter, for she had to marry someone that her parents had selected.

A. Whomever

B. Whatever

C. Whoever was

D. Whoever was that

A   B   C   D

3. _____ the ozone layer has already thinned to   **A**   **B**   **C**   **D**

a dangerous point is a serious problem.

A. What

B. That

C. It is a fact that

D. Scientists know that

4. It is clear _____ the city government will have   **A**   **B**   **C**   **D**

to raise taxes if the police force is going to be strengthened.

A. what

B. that

C. whatever

D. whether

5. It is generally considered unwise to give a child   **A**   **B**   **C**   **D**

_____ he or she wants.

A. whatever is it

B. that

C. whatever that

D. whatever

6. Organic food companies stress _____ no   **A**   **B**   **C**   **D**

pesticides or other harmful products are used in growing

their products.

A. what

B. neither

C. both

D. that

7. After the flood had left so many homeless, the neighboring towns-

people donated _____ of their food, clothing

and shelter.

A. however could they spare

B. whichever they can spare

C. whatever they could spare

D. what they spared

A   B   C   D

8. Both gubernatorial candidates are well qualified, so that

_____ will serve the state well.

A. whom is elected

B. whomever is elected

C. whoever is elected

D. whichever elects

A   B   C   D

9. _____ the mathematical ability of girls is

innately the same as that of boys has still not been universally

accepted.

A. It is a fact that

B. In fact,

C. The fact that

D. The fact is that

A   B   C   D

10. Dermatologists are recommending that people with fair skin

_____ a strong sun screen.

A. use

B. that they use

C. to use

D. are using

A   B   C   D

PART TWO

DIRECTIONS: Each sentence has four underlined words or phrases. The four underlined parts of the sentence are marked A, B, C, and D. Circle the letter of the <u>one</u> underlined word or phrase that is NOT CORRECT.

Example:

People in <u>every part</u> of the world now <u>readily</u> and easily
       A   B
<u>communicates</u> <u>by means</u> of electronic mail.
  C   D

            A   B   Ⓒ   D

11. <u>That</u> spurred the great explorations of the fifteenth and sixteenth   A   B   C   D
    A
    centuries was the <u>desire to find</u> <u>a more</u> expeditious route to
                      B   C
    <u>the spice</u> supplies of the Far East.
      D

12. Market researchers find out exactly <u>how many</u> <u>people live</u> in a   A   B   C   D
                             A   B
    certain area and <u>what</u> <u>are their spending habits</u>.
               C   D

13. The belief <u>what</u> a person <u>gets</u> what he or she <u>deserves</u> in this   A   B   C   D
             A   B   C
    world <u>persists</u> despite evidence to the contrary.
        D

14. Urban sprawl occurred <u>wherever</u> <u>the population expanded</u>   A   B   C   D
                      A   B
    rapidly and <u>where</u> <u>were there</u> no comprehensive plans for
             C   D
    dealing with the situation.

15. <u>What is clear</u> is the <u>fact that</u> the mediocre level of popular   A   B   C   D
     A   B
    television programming is based on <u>what do</u> advertisers think
                           C
    <u>the viewers want</u> to see.
        D

16. In spite of <u>the fact that</u> doctors have recommended strongly <u>that</u> A   B   C   D
              A   B
    adults <u>refrained</u> <u>from smoking</u> near children, such warnings have
          C   D
    largely gone unheeded.

17. <u>Whatever</u> the individuals felt before attending the group therapy A   B   C   D
     A
    sessions, <u>it was clear</u> <u>that</u> <u>did they leave</u> the course with renewed
            B   C   D
    hope.

18. The coach insists that the players <u>do</u> <u>whatever</u> <u>it is</u> necessary
                                    A   B   C

<u>to win</u> the game.
 D

                                  A   B   C   D

19. The demonstrators for prison reform <u>demanded</u> that all the
                                        A

inequities of the system <u>were</u> <u>addressed</u> <u>before the day ended</u>.
                         B   C   D

A   B   C   D

20. The problem with the new, more equitable income taxes <u>is</u>
                                         A

<u>because</u> they don't satisfy <u>demands that</u> all possible loopholes
 B   C

<u>be eliminated</u>.
 D

A   B   C   D

TEST: UNITS 20–21

PART ONE

DIRECTIONS: Circle the letter of the correct answer to complete each sentence.

Example:

Dolphins, _____ porpoises, are well known for   A   B   (C)   D

their ability to delight humans with their antics.

  A. alike

  B. that they are like

  C. like

  D. which are alike

1. Without the help of the Indians of the area, the Pilgrims in   A   B   C   D

    Massachusetts _____ able to celebrate their

    first Thanksgiving.

  A. would never had been

  B. would never have been

  C. had never been

  D. they were never

2. Had the Spanish remained in North America, Canadians and   A   B   C   D

    Americans _____ Spanish now instead of English.

  A. would have spoken

  B. would be speaking

  C. have been speaking

  D. had been speaking

3. Corporate interests would not have voted for the Republican

candidate if _____ considerable tax

reductions.

    A   B   C   D

A. she did not promise

B. she had not promised

C. she hasn't promised

D. she were not to promise

4. It is clear that John didn't make a good impression at his job

interview; if so, the firm _____ him by now.

    A   B   C   D

A. would call

B. would called

C. call

D. would have called

5. Although having difficulty in obtaining a license to operate a

cable television channel, the station owners still hope that they

_____ one this year.

    A   B   C   D

A. will procure

B. would procure

C. were to procure

D. have procured

6. The crash victims probably would have died _____

arrived at the scene of the accident within minutes of its occurrence.

    A   B   C   D

A. if had the ambulance not

B. did the ambulance not

C. if the ambulance would not have

D. had the ambulance not

7. Travel films have long been popular among people who would   A   B   C   D

like to travel around the world and wish _____

the money to do so.

A. they have

B. they will have

C. they had

D. had they had

8. In certain types of mental illness, when a person speaks   A   B   C   D

_____ a king, he truly believes that he is a king

even if he is, in reality, a working man.

A. if he is

B. as though he be

C. as he was

D. as though he were

9. It is essential that _____ enough rain before   A   B   C   D

the month ends if the area is to produce adequate coffee crops.

A. there be

B. there have

C. there should be

D. it has

10. A peaceful demonstration is anticipated, but the riot squad will   A   B   C   D

remain ready to act _____ .

A. if should occur unexpected violence

B. that unexpected violence occurs

C. should unexpected violence occur

D. were to occur unexpected violence

PART TWO

DIRECTIONS: Each sentence has four underlined words or phrases. The four underlined parts of the sentence are marked A, B, C, and D. Circle the letter of the <u>one</u> underlined word or phrase that is NOT CORRECT.

Example:

People in <u>every part</u> of the world now <u>readily</u> and easily
         A   B
<u>communicates</u> <u>by means</u> of electronic mail.
  C   D

A   B   Ⓒ   D

11. <u>If environmental groups</u> <u>have not exerted</u> pressure, <u>it is</u> almost
        A   B   C
certain that pandas <u>would now be</u> extinct.
                 D

A   B   C   D

12. Many people <u>have expressed</u> the concern <u>that a</u> problem <u>should</u>
               A   B   C
<u>develop</u> at a nuclear facility, the results <u>would be</u> disastrous.
                             D

A   B   C   D

13. <u>It was</u> fortunate for the actress <u>that she had</u> already worked
    A   B
with the director; otherwise, she <u>will</u> never <u>have been</u> awarded
                           C   D
the leading role.

A   B   C   D

14. Many people <u>buying</u> lottery tickets every week <u>believe</u> that if
             A   B
only they <u>have</u> a lot of money, their lives <u>would be</u> perfect.
        C   D

A   B   C   D

15. If the president <u>were become</u> incapacitated, specific constitutional
                A
procedures to install the vice president <u>would have to be</u> implemented
                                   B
quickly <u>so that</u> the leadership of the country <u>would remain</u> intact.
        C   D

A   B   C   D

16. In the days of the American pioneer, <u>it was</u> vital that the wagons
                                A
<u>crossing</u> the great prairies <u>carry</u> guns; otherwise, the occupants
 B   C
<u>had been</u> helpless against wild animals or attacks by Indians.
  D

A   B   C   D

17. <u>Many a spirited</u> young person <u>who plays</u> practical jokes in his
    A   B
teens later <u>wishes that</u> he <u>has behaved</u> in a more mature manner.
          C   D

A   B   C   D

18. Queen Elizabeth <u>would never have</u> become <u>the</u> queen of England
                            A   B

    <u>if had not her uncle</u>, Edward VIII, renounced the throne <u>to marry</u>
              C   D

    a commoner.

           A   B   C   D

19. <u>By suggesting</u> that a softer approach toward the <u>opposing</u> party
       A   B

    <u>were adopted</u>, the lawyer hoped <u>to effect</u> a decent settlement for
       C   D

    his client.

           A   B   C   D

20. <u>Had the South</u> <u>defeated</u> the North in the American Civil War in
        A   B

    1865, the industrial development of the country <u>would proceed</u>
                                          C

    more slowly than <u>it did</u>.
                    D

           A   B   C   D

ANSWER KEY FOR TEST: UNITS 1–3

Note: Correct responses for Part Two questions appear in parentheses.

PART ONE

1. C **2.** A **3.** C **4.** B **5.** A **6.** C **7.** D **8.** C **9.** A **10.** B

PART TWO

11. B (survive) **12.** A (have been eroding) **13.** B (was) **14.** C (have watched)
15. B (may have originated) **16.** C (introduced) **17.** A (come) **18.** D (listen)
19. D (might be hungry) **20.** D (would never be)

ANSWER KEY FOR TEST: UNITS 4–7

PART ONE

1. B **2.** B **3.** B **4.** D **5.** D **6.** C **7.** B **8.** C **9.** D **10.** C

PART TWO

11. A (Horse races) **12.** C (all of their) **13.** D (of words) **14.** C (the first five)
15. B (medical) **16.** C (the oldest of) **17.** B (a new) **18.** C (baseball)
19. C (the only country) **20.** B (of coffee)

ANSWER KEY FOR TEST: UNITS 8–9

PART ONE

1. C **2.** A **3.** B **4.** D **5.** C **6.** B **7.** A **8.** B **9.** C **10.** B

PART TWO

11. B (it is considered) **12.** C (was hunted) **13.** B (purchased by the East India Company)
14. C (is found) **15.** D (killed) **16.** D (never been proved/proven)
17. A (have been predicted) **18.** C (painted) **19.** B (had to shout)
20. B (must have been committed)

ANSWER KEY FOR TEST: UNITS 10–11

PART ONE

1. B **2.** D **3.** C **4.** C **5.** D **6.** B **7.** C **8.** A **9.** C **10.** C

PART TWO

11. A (to make) **12.** B (to paint) **13.** C (smoking) **14.** B (to emigrate)
15. B (be considered) **16.** D (applauding) **17.** C (eat) **18.** A (make)
19. C (achieve) **20.** A (being considered)

ANSWER KEY FOR TEST: UNITS 12–15

PART ONE

1. C **2.** B **3.** B **4.** B **5.** C **6.** B **7.** A **8.** D **9.** C **10.** D

PART TWO

11. B (did Columbus) **12.** B (only a few) **13.** D (because) **14.** B (so convenient)
15. B (has the supply of mahogany) **16.** C (writer) **17.** A (When [he was] first setting foot)
18. A (Having retired) **19.** A (Although) **20.** A (Reflecting)

ANSWER KEY FOR TEST: UNITS 16–17

PART ONE

1. D **2.** C **3.** D **4.** C **5.** C **6.** D **7.** D **8.** D **9.** A **10.** D

PART TWO

11. D (containing/that contain/which contain) **12.** B (which is) **13.** A (is spoken)
14. B (who has) **15.** A (half of whom) **16.** C (who was) **17.** B (means)
18. C (resisting) **19.** A (0—omit *which*) **20.** B (in which/where)

ANSWER KEY FOR TEST: UNITS 18–19

PART ONE

1. A   **2.** A   **3.** B   **4.** B   **5.** D   **6.** D   **7.** C   **8.** C   **9.** C   **10.** A

PART TWO

11. A (What)   **12.** D (their spending habits are)   **13.** A (that)   **14.** D (there were)
15. C (what)   **16.** C (refrain)   **17.** D (they left)   **18.** C (is)   **19.** B (be)   **20.** B (that)

ANSWER KEY FOR TEST: UNITS 20–21

PART ONE

1. B   **2.** B   **3.** B   **4.** D   **5.** A   **6.** D   **7.** C   **8.** D   **9.** A   **10.** C

PART TWO

11. B (had not exerted)   **12.** B (that if a)   **13.** C (would)   **14.** C (had)
15. A (were to become)   **16.** D (would have been)   **17.** D (had behaved)
18. C (had not her uncle)   **19.** C (be adopted)   **20.** C (would have proceded)